The DIRECTORY *of*
Quilting
TECHNIQUES

The DIRECTORY *of*
Quilting
TECHNIQUES

Caroline Rodrigues

CHARTWELL
BOOKS, INC.

First published in 2006 by

CHARTWELL BOOKS INC.

A Division of Book Sales Inc.

114 Northfield Avenue

Edison, New Jersey 08837

ISBN-13: 978-0-7858-2015-4
ISBN-10: 0-7858-2015-9

This book was conceived,
designed, and produced by

THE IVY PRESS LIMITED

The Old Candlemakers

Lewes, East Sussex BN7 2NZ

Creative Director: Peter Bridgewater
Publisher: Sophie Collins
Editorial Director: Jason Hook
Art Director: Karl Shanahan
Design: The Lanaways
Illustrators: Peters & Zabransky, Kate Simunek
Mac Illustrator: Lyndsey Godden
Project Editor: Mandy Greenfield

Printed and bound in China

Contents

Introduction

Welcome to *The Directory of Quilting Techniques*. This book will lead you step by step through all the skills you need to create your own quilts and, even if you are a beginner, you will soon be quilting confidently. All the instructions you will need are here, together with inspirational designs and a range of templates to copy. Once you get started you'll realize why quilters get so hooked on this wonderful craft.

Quilting developed from practical necessity. Its fabric layers, stuffed with a warm filling and stitched for security, were ideal for producing warm clothing and bedding. Yet quilting has developed into something very beautiful—no longer just a craft, but an art form, where the patterns, colors, and rows of stitches may be handed down from previous generations, but the artistic input comes from you. Give it a try— you'll find that the design element comes naturally and that you are creating a unique work of art that reflects your personality.

It's easy to get started; just collect some scrap fabrics, thread a needle, and you're ready. Quilting is the perfect hobby for busy people. You can take pieces in your bag to stitch by hand on journeys or whenever you have a spare moment.

Begin by learning how to piece together a simple patchwork block, then progress to trying out the different types of patchwork, from straightforward log cabin designs *(see pages 70–74)* to intricate cathedral windows *(see pages 92–97).* Try your hand at the varied methods of appliqué *(see pages 113–138).* And consider whether to adorn your quilt with hand or machine quilting, in simple lines or complex patterns *(see pages 139–180).*

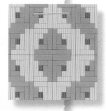

ORIGINS

Patchwork had its beginnings in ancient times, when it was used to make warm bedding and garments, although we have no surviving examples of this early craft. By the Middle Ages quilted fabrics were being used as padding underneath armor. The earliest English patchwork quilts may have been made of wool (the most abundant fabric of the time), though the oldest-surviving English example, dated 1708, was made from chintz imported from India. Using paper templates for piecing was a typical method and, when the papers were left

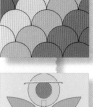

in place, they provide an interesting way of dating a quilt. The American Saltonstall quilt, which was pieced with papers from the local newspaper, was dated to 1704, thanks to this method.

In North America quilting developed as a way to teach young girls the sewing skills they would need when caring for and clothing their own families. With each quilt they completed, their proficiency developed. There are few quilts dated before 1800, although it is certain quilts were being made before this time. By the nineteenth century the skill was widespread, and in the late 1800s a fashion for crazy quilts developed. These were made from velvets, silks, cottons, and wools and were embellished with lace, embroidery, beads, and silk flowers. By the early twentieth century Americans had a passion for patchwork quilting, with fairs and competitions, while magazines printed numerous articles and patterns.

There are so many quilting techniques to try, and so many variations in working them. You'll find that not all quilters do things the same way—and that's fine. From your first steps as a novice quilter you're joining a worldwide family with generations of stitchcraft to draw on.

Hawaiian appliqué

EQUIPMENT AND
BASIC TECHNIQUES

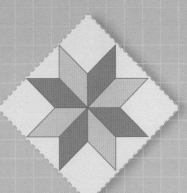

EQUIPMENT AND
BASIC TECHNIQUES

It's easy to get started with patchwork. You need a

minimum of tools and equipment, most of which you may

already have at home, such as pencils and sharp scissors.

Once you progress, you can gradually add to your collection.

The basic techniques are easy to master. If you can sew

running stitch by hand, or manage a straight stitch on

a sewing machine, you are ready to embark on your

first patchwork project without delay.

The outer circle shows colors in their purest form.

The middle circle shows shades and tones.

The inner circle shows the pastel tones of colors.

Fabric and color

Most quilters use 100 percent cotton fabrics, though silks and wools can also be used to obtain special effects. Cottons don't fray as much as synthetics, hold a crease when pressed, and aren't as slippery as synthetics. They are also easy to handle, drape well, and tend to be less transparent, so that seam allowances do not show as much from the right side.

COLOR

Though workmanship and design are important, it is the colors you pick for a quilt that give it instant impact. The color wheel is a useful tool for learning about combining colors to achieve the effects you want. On the wheel the primary colors of red, blue, and yellow are equidistant from each other, while the secondary colors (made by combining two of the primaries) sit between the primary colors—for example, the primaries blue and red make the secondary color of violet. The tertiary colors make up the rest of the wheel, and are made from a mix of the colors that lie adjacent to them. Notice how the warm reds, oranges, and yellows all fall on one side of the wheel, and the cooler blues and greens on the other.

On the outside of the wheel, the colors are shown in their purest, most intense form, but there are many variations in value and intensity (some of which are shown in

Blues and greens recede into the background while red appears to advance.

A mix of blue and yellow creates green.

the inner circles). Mixing opposites from the color wheel will add contrast and highlights to your patchwork.

It's quite possible to make up a quilt in intense, primary colors, and some people do so. However, thanks to the many variations in value, intensity, tints, shades, and tones, a patchworker has just as many colors to choose from as an artist.

VALUE
The value of a color is its shade—whether it is lighter or darker. By working with different values and just one color, you could make a monochromatic quilt solely in blues, for example, that still includes remarkable variety.

A mix of red and yellow creates orange.

INTENSITY
Although the outer color wheel shows intense colors, these can be diluted to give duller shades, or tones, that are more relaxing to look at. Varying intensity is an important part of designing a quilt, because using solely intense shades can have a jarring effect.

CREATING TINTS, SHADES, AND TONES
Taking a pure color and adding white creates a tint. Adding black gives a shade. Adding white and black (gray) creates a tone.

A mix of blue and red creates purple.

Primary

Secondary

Tertiary

Complementary

Harmonious

Cool

Warm

Pastel

ADVANCING AND RECEDING COLORS

Once you realize that some colors advance (or stand out from a background) while others recede (or blend with it), your quilts will be richer and more inventive. Dark, pure, and warm colors are strong and vibrant and tend to advance, while light, toned-down, or cool colors tend to recede and create a relaxing, soothing mood.

To include variety and excitement in a quilting block, use just a small amount of a strong color that will stand out against the other colors.

DIAGRAM 1
Contrasting colors, which come from opposite sides of the color wheel, spell out drama and excitement.

DIAGRAM 2
Harmonious color schemes use colors that are close to each other on the color wheel to create a restful effect.

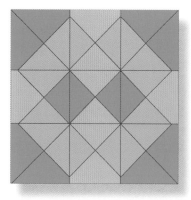

PRACTICING COLOR TECHNIQUES

Try drawing out blocks on graph paper and coloring them in different ways to emphasize various parts of the design. Experiment with both harmonious and contrasting colors, and try out different tints and shades to see what effects you get.

DIAGRAM 1
In this colorway a square on point seems to advance from behind a grid.

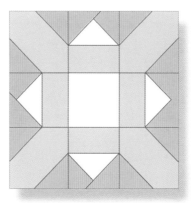

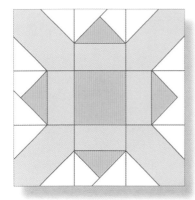

DIAGRAM 2
Reverse the colors and the square is less dominant.

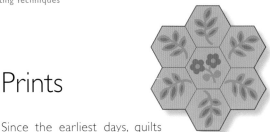

Prints

Since the earliest days, quilts have included printed patterns. These are a complicated addition to a quilt, because you need to choose them not only for color, but for value, intensity, and scale. The best way to appraise them is to stand back and see whether the pattern merges into one, in which case you can judge it for value and intensity (see page 13).

Use stripes to emphasize geometric patterns.

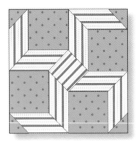

MAKE A DESIGN WALL

Use a large noticeboard, or cover a foam board with white cotton flannel, to pin up patches as you work. This way you can see how the colors of your design are working together, before they are actually pieced.

• A large and readily visible print can be striking if it is positioned carefully, or you can use its motif for appliqué.

• A medium-scale print may have regular-sized motifs and a background pattern, making it interesting to use.

• Small-scale prints are easy to work with.

• Tone-on-tone prints—made from one color, but varying tones—have small motifs that almost disappear when viewed from a distance.

• Floral prints are indispensable for adding charm to the geometric shape of blocks.

• Geometric prints, stripes, dots, and plaids can be cut in ways that emphasize their pattern when the pieces are stitched together. Stripes cut and pieced in the right way, for instance, can form chevrons.

• "Conversational prints" include fun motifs of animals or objects, which are good for blocks or for appliqué.

It's easy to move patches around a design wall before making a final decision.

Backing and batting

The filling for a quilt, which gives it softness and three-dimensional quality, is known as batting. There are various types to choose from.

- Polyester batting is easiest to quilt, particularly in the thin 2oz (60g) version. It may "beard"—transferring fine fibers to the quilt top—but close quilting will prevent this.
- Cotton batting is easier to machine quilt than hand quilt, but the needle-punched version makes hand quilting easier.
- A cotton and polyester mix is easy to stitch and need not be as closely quilted as cotton batting.
- Wool batting drapes well and retains its springiness.
- Silk batting is sometimes used to match a silk quilt top.
- Domette is a woven interlining, which is good for wall hangings that require a flatter look.

BACKING

Choose a backing of similar weight to your quilt top, and with the same fiber content. If you will be quilting through the backing, choose a cotton fabric that is easy to stitch through. Backing fabric in extra-wide widths means that you need not piece the backing together.

Threads, needles, and sewing machines

A patchworker is only as good as his or her tools, so make sure you're stitching with the right needle and threads to suit your quilting project.

THREADS

For hand or machine piecing, use cotton sewing thread on cotton fabrics (polyester and silk threads are also available). The higher the thread number, the finer it is, while the strength increases with the number of plies (or strands).

When hand quilting, use 100 percent cotton quilting thread, because it is thicker, tightly spun, and strong enough to hold the layers together. For decorative quilting and appliqué, try metallic, crochet, embroidery, and perle cotton threads.

Buy tacking cotton for basting.

thread varieties

There are many different decorative threads to choose from, as well as the standard cotton used for joining patches.

Tip Buy cotton thread in neutral colors on large spools for machine work—it's much more economical.

NEEDLES

For hand piecing, use needles called "sharps." The higher the number, the smaller the needle. Size 8 or 9 is ideal, but buy a mixed pack of sharps and try them out. Sharps are also good for tacking a quilt together, as are millinery (straw) needles or fine long darners. For appliqué, fine sharps are preferred.

When hand quilting, use needles known as "betweens." These short, strong needles move easily through the layers of a quilt. Sizes 9, 10, and 12 are ideal.

For machine piecing a size 80/12 machine needle is best, and when you are machine quilting, work with a larger needle than usual.

PINS

Use straight pins (size 0.6mm) for pinning patches for hand or machine piecing. Choose the larger-head ones when putting quilt layers together, because they are easy to spot and won't get left behind, or try long 2in (5cm) pins or safety pins. Tiny "Lills" pins are useful for appliqué. Replace pins when they become blunt.

SEWING MACHINES

A basic sewing machine will piece and quilt projects fast, and you just need to master straightforward stitching for patchwork and quilting, and zigzag for appliqué. An even-feed foot (also called a "walking foot") is useful, and so is a

"little foot," giving an exact ¼in (6mm) seam allowance. A "big foot" or a darning foot gives you a good view when you are quilting. A transparent foot is helpful for embroidery, and a braiding foot for couching.

For free-motion quilting, a machine that lets you lower the feed dogs (the flat cogs that feed the fabric through as you sew) is a definite plus.

Cutting tools

You will need different cutting tools for different purposes; the ones described below are recommended.

SCISSORS

Good, sharp scissors are invaluable for the quilter. Make sure you have several pairs: one sharp pair used only for fabric; another, older pair for cutting paper or template plastic; and a pair of small embroidery scissors for getting into tight corners (ensure that they cut sharply, right up to the points).

SNAP-BLADE KNIFE

A snap-blade knife (X-Acto) with a retractable blade is advisable if you want to cut your own stencils and templates from template plastic. For quilting stencils, use a double-bladed X-Acto knife, which cuts $\frac{1}{16}$in (1.5mm) channels. An electric hot stencil cutter does the same job.

ROTARY CUTTER

This invaluable, small, sharp cutting wheel mounted in a holder slices through layers of fabric, enabling you to cut accurate strips, squares, and patches. Rotary cutters come in three sizes. Most have a straight handle for use by left- and right-handers, while cutters with a curved handle can be reassembled for left-handers. All have snap on/off guards, or an automatic retractable guard. Replace the blade regularly. Rotary cutters are used with self-healing cutting mats and acrylic rulers (see *opposite*).

Use sharp scissors for accuracy and a rotary cutter for speed.

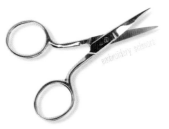

Quilting helpmates

You probably won't need everything on this list, but here are some handy helpmates. You can add to your basic kit as you get more experienced.

- Acrylic rulers and drafting triangles: Quilters' rulers are marked with a measuring grid for rotary cutting or measuring; drafting triangles are useful for checking that right angles on templates are exact.
- Basting gun: This inserts plastic tacks to hold a quilt sandwich together.
- Beeswax: Run your thread through this to strengthen it and prevent tangling.
- Bias square: You can use this acrylic square instead of a ruler when rotary cutting.
- Cutting mat: A mat is essential for rotary cutting, with a grid of either inches or centimeters. Buy a large one, and store it flat so that it cannot warp.
- Hoops and frames: See pages 152–153 for advice on wooden hoops, tubular frames, and floor frames.
- Masking tape: Use this to mark quilt lines and to hold template plastic or quilt backing in place. Choose a low-tack version to avoid leaving sticky marks.
- Press bars: Run a bias strip through a press bar to fold the tape ready for use in stained-glass patchwork.
- Quarter seamer: Use this to mark a ¼in (6mm) seam allowance.
- Thimble: Choose a metal, plastic, or leather one.

Accurate measuring is essential for patchwork, so make sure you've got the right tools.

acrylic ruler

masking tape

beeswax

thimbles

drafting triangles

COMPANION ANGLE™
designed by Darlene Zimmerman

EZ INTERNATIONAL
95 Mayhill St. Seaside Brook NJ 07060

Paper, pencils, and more

You'll need pencils and fabric markers and, if you intend to design your own patchwork, you'll also require graph paper and template plastic.

- Pencils: Get some H and HB pencils, plus silver, yellow, or white pencils for marking designs.
- Soapstone markers: These are useful because you can wash the marks out with soap and water.
- Chalk: This shows up well on dark fabrics and brushes off easily.
- Blue, water-soluble markers: Useful, but do not iron the marks before washing or they will persist.
- Air-soluble pens: The marks made by these pens are visible for up to 12 hours.
- Graph paper (square and isometric): For designing your own patchwork.
- Tracing paper and freezer paper: To transfer your designs to fabric.
- Templates (with or without seam allowance): For hand piecing or machine work.
- Quilting stencils: These have channels for marking your design on the fabric.
- Template plastic: For cutting out stencils.
- Compasses, a protractor, and a flexicurve: These are needed to mark angles and curves.

Choose a selection of colors to show up on different fabric backgrounds.

Designing patchwork

Patchwork designs are easy to come by, from quilts, books of block designs (and there are some block examples on pages 58–61), or patterns from nature. Try drafting your own blocks, too. Specialized computer programs will let you design at high speed, repeating a block, recoloring it, rotating it, and reversing it to see its possibilities.

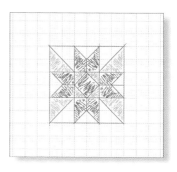

DRAWING SHAPES
Use squared graph paper (*right*) for drafting square, triangular, rectangular, or log cabin designs. Use isometric paper (marked with triangles, *below right*) for hexagons, triangles, stars, trapezoids, and diamonds.

DRAWING A BLOCK
Patchwork blocks are made up of a grid of equal-sized squares, which can be subdivided into smaller shapes. The block may be divisible into four patches, or into nine or more squares.

Use a measurement for the overall block size that can be divided evenly by one row of units within the block. For example, if you are working with a five-patch block (containing 25 squares in rows of 5), choosing a 10in block size works, because 10 divided by 5 = 2. The 2in squares will be easy to measure and cut.

Draw out the block, then map out your design within it. Make photocopies and color them in various ways to make the design stand out.

Working with templates

Templates are copies of pattern pieces, which can be drawn around onto paper to mark out the shape you need to cut. There are many ready-made templates that you can buy, or you can make your own from template plastic. The more often you intend to use the template, the more robust it should be. For appliqué designs you may only want to use a template once, in which case it can be cut from freezer paper rather than template plastic.

Tip It's a good idea to color-code homemade templates according to size with markers or stickers, so that you can quickly find the template you need.

READY-MADE TEMPLATES

Templates for machine piecing include a ¼in (6mm) seam allowance. Cut them along the solid line and stitch along the dotted line. Templates for hand piecing or appliqué do not have a seam allowance, and you need to add your own.

A window template (*left*) allows you to mark the seam line and the cutting line. It is a good way of selecting fabrics for use in a project, because you can place it on the fabric and see immediately how the cut patches will look.

TEMPLATE CHOICES

Templates and their sister stencils come in packs to suit different projects.

- Sets of templates for making popular blocks: These save you the trouble of drawing and cutting out your own templates.
- Sets of assorted shapes, such as triangles and squares in various sizes: These are useful for making many blocks.
- Templates for English piecing: These consist of a metal template to use for the papers and a plastic or metal window template for the fabric.
- Sheets of template plastic: These are printed with a wide selection of shapes.
- Acrylic shapes: These are used with a rotary cutter for machine sewing.
- Stencils with a selection of different-sized slots: These can be used to mark varied sizes of diamonds or clamshells.
- Rubber stamps in various shapes: These are for inking and marking fabrics.

The stencils below left have slots through which to draw.

Enlarging designs and cutting templates

Tip If you are using a rotary cutter, keep a blade reserved solely for plastic.

You can enlarge a design on graph paper or isometric paper, or you can use a photocopier. If you rely on a photocopier, be sure to check the resulting designs with a ruler or set square, to ensure that the sizes are absolutely accurate.

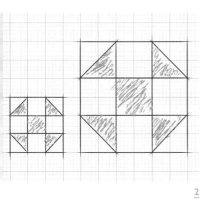

1 Use the squares on geometric paper, or the triangles on isometric paper, to mark out the lines of your design.

2 Count out the number of squares, then redraw the design by doubling the number of squares or multiplying by the desired number to get the size you require.

_2_

3 Trace the shapes onto template plastic, and add a ¼in (6mm) seam allowance.

4 Place the template plastic on your cutting mat. Use a craft knife or a rotary cutter and ruler to cut out the shapes, paying great attention to accuracy.

Tip Blunt the ends of long, pointed shapes such as diamonds before making the templates.

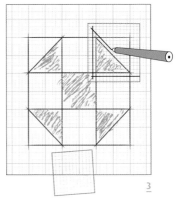

_3_

Using templates

Draw very carefully around the templates onto the fabric, because if you distort the fabric or your marked line is inaccurate, the patches won't stitch together correctly.

Tip Stop templates from slipping on fabric by gluing some sandpaper to the back.

Place the templates on the wrong side of the fabric for marking patchwork patches; on the right side for appliqué or quilting. Place the longest edge of each piece on the straight grain (parallel with the selvage). Place clamshells or Dresden plate designs so that the straight grain runs vertically through the templates.

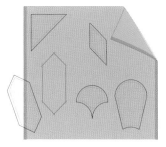

2 Mark around the fabric using a sharp pencil or a fabric marking pen. Cut out the shape with sharp scissors, following the marked line exactly.

MARKING OUT ROWS OF PIECES

Templates for hand piecing do not include a seam allowance, so you need to draw shapes with a gap between them. You can mark on the cutting line or, if you are brave, judge it by eye. Templates for machine piecing can be lined up without any gaps, matching the cutting lines.

Templates

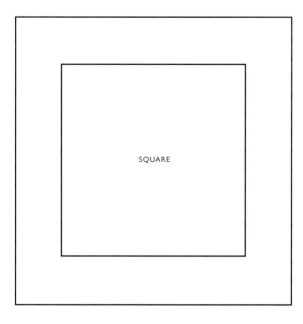

SQUARE

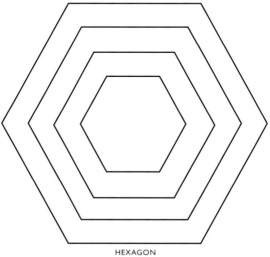

HEXAGON

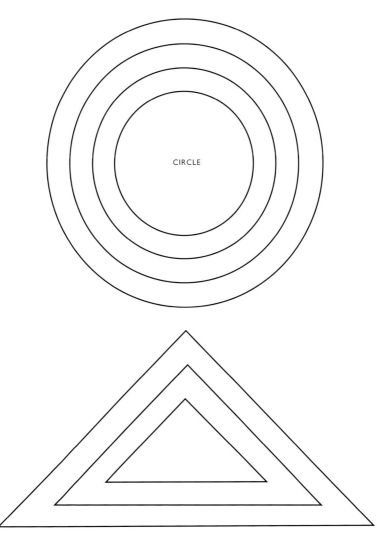

CIRCLE

RIGHT-ANGLED TRIANGLE

Templates

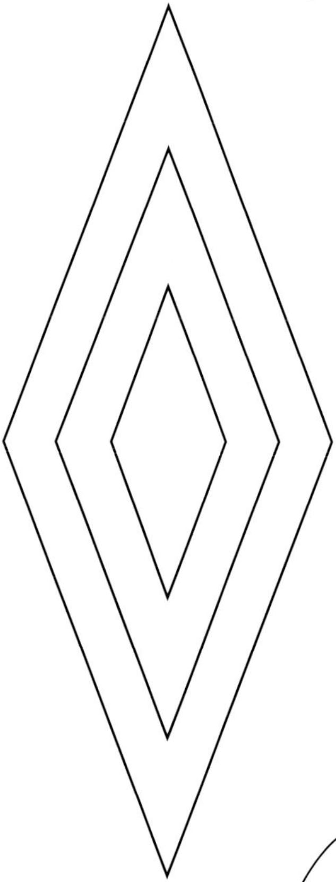

LONG DIAMOND

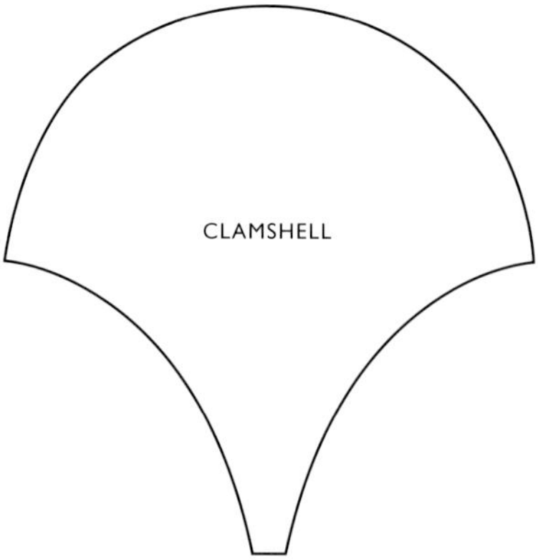

CLAMSHELL

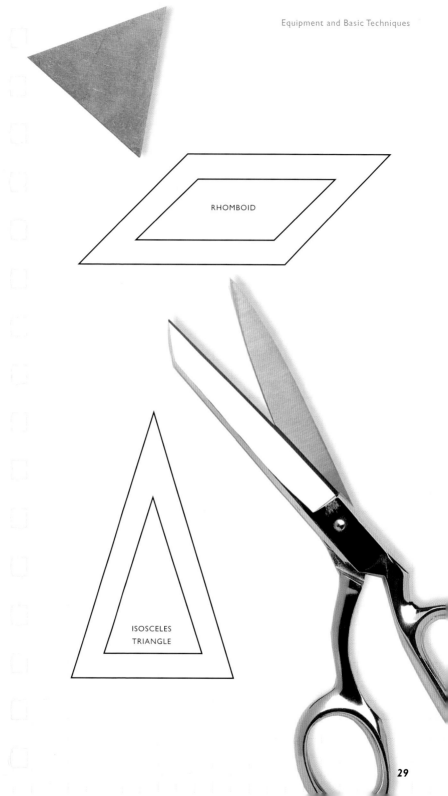

RHOMBOID

ISOSCELES
TRIANGLE

Templates

DRESDEN PLATE

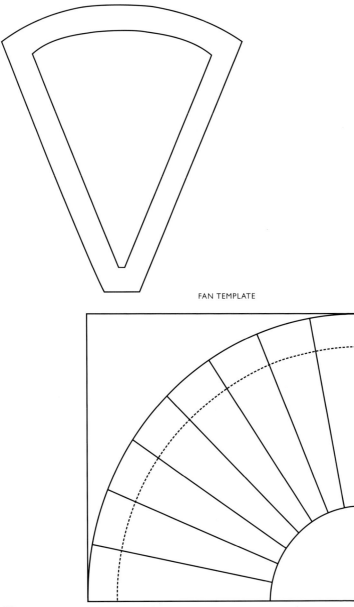

FAN TEMPLATE

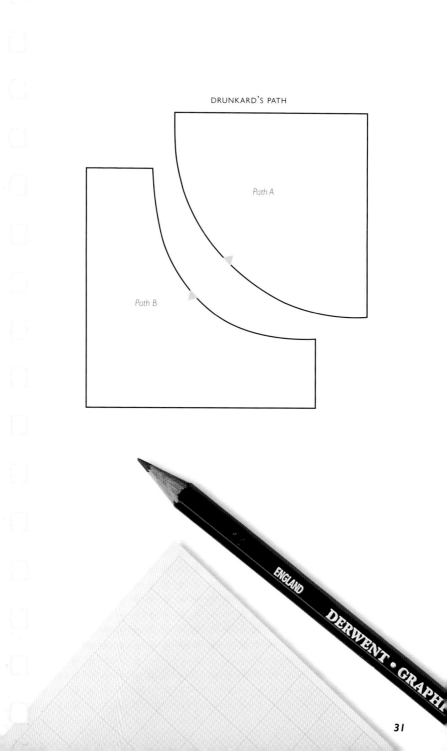

DRUNKARD'S PATH

Path A

Path B

Preparing fabrics

A finished quilt is the result of hours of labor, so if you intend to wash the quilt in future, it may be wise to wash the fabrics first. Bear in mind the following points.

FABRIC COATINGS
The coating that stiffens fabrics also makes them easier to cut and mark. If you wash fabrics, you can reintroduce the stiffness using a spray starch.

WASHING FABRICS
Sort fabrics into piles of light and dark, then wash them in warm water with mild soap rather than detergent. When they are dry, iron the fabric.

DYE PROBLEMS
To check whether a fabric "bleeds" (that is, whether the dye runs), wash a fabric sample and dry it on some paper towels. If the dye transfers to the paper, soak the fabric in three parts cold water to one part white vinegar, or use a specialized dye-retaining product, then test again.

SHRINKAGE
Cottons and other natural fibers, unless they are pretreated, shrink when washed, particularly on the first wash. Ironing can reduce some of this shrinkage. Combining washed and unwashed fabrics in a project can result in puckered seams.

The fun of quilting is in the selection of a good variety of fabrics.

Press seams as you go—a good iron is absolutely essential.

Cutting fabrics

Make sure your scissors stay sharp by using one pair for fabrics only. Reserve a separate pair for cutting paper and template plastic.

1 Mark strips or shapes on the wrong side of one fabric. Place layers of fabric (six at most), wrong side up, on an ironing board, pressing each layer. Put the marked fabric on top.

2 Pin the fabrics within each marked segment, without disturbing the fabric layers. Cut them into strips, then into pieces. (To cut mirror image pieces, place the layers alternately right and wrong side up.)

_2_

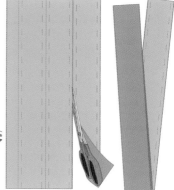

3 To cut long fabric strips, lay out the fabric and, following the fabric grain, mark the width of your strips, including a ¼in (6mm) seam allowance on each side.

4 Join the marks with a ruler. Use a ¼in (6mm) seamer to mark seam allowances with dotted lines. Cut out along the solid lines.

Using a rotary cutter

Instead of laboriously cutting out patches with scissors, you can use a rotary cutter to make strips and shapes in no time at all. The labor-saving rotary cutter consists of a circular blade fixed in a holder, used on a cutting mat that will not blunt the blade.

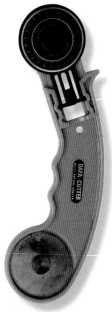

rotary cutter

EQUIPMENT REQUIRED

You will need a medium or large rotary cutter, a 24 × 18in (60 × 46cm) cutting mat, two 24 × 6in (60 × 16cm) acrylic rulers, and a 6in (16cm) bias square. The equipment is sold in imperial or metric sizes (not both together); quilters usually tend to work in imperial measurements.

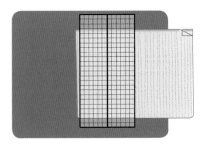

1 Fold the fabric in half on the cutting mat, with the selvages matching at the top, and the fold at the bottom. Place two rulers on the mat, matching the horizontal lines marked on them with the fold of the fabric.

2 Move the rulers to the left, so that the right-hand edge of the left ruler just covers all the raw edges of the fabric. Remove the right ruler. Press down on the remaining ruler, spreading out your fingers, then run the blade of the rotary cutter along the edge of the ruler, away from you.

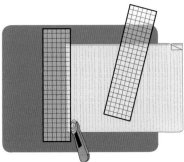

Rotary tips

• *Use the ruler to measure, rather than relying on the printed measurements on the cutting mat.*

• *Walk your fingers along the ruler when you are cutting long strips.*

• *Get into the habit of locking the cutter after every cut.*

• *Stand up so that you can put more pressure on the ruler.*

• *Change the rotary cutter blade regularly.*

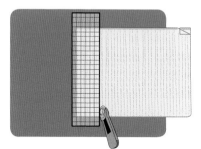

3 Place one ruler on the fabric, matching a vertical line on the ruler to the cut edge of the fabric, and measuring off the desired strip width on the ruler. Cut as before.

4 Open out the strip and check that your cutting is even. Use the ruler to cut the strips into squares or other shapes, and the bias square to cut triangles.

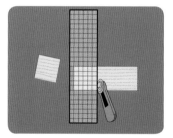

Hand sewing

There's something comforting about sewing by hand, and it is the traditional method of making patchwork. The very fact that it is slow allows for great accuracy. Work with a sharps needle. Try to match the color of the thread with the predominant color in your quilt, or choose a neutral tone (beige and gray are good).

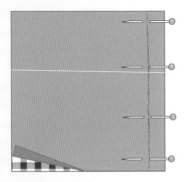 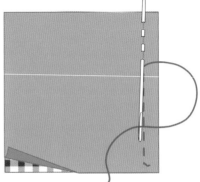

| Pin the patches right sides
together, matching the edges and corners. Mark the seam allowance and insert pins at right angles to the marked line.

2 Starting and finishing ¼in (6mm) from the edges, make a knot and a backstitch for extra security. Then work running stitch along the seam line, rocking the needle to pick up several stitches at a time. Catch the thread end in the first stitches as you start. Finish with a backstitch, then whip the needle back through the previous stitches before cutting the thread.

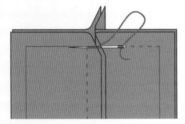

3 When joining rows together you will have to stitch across previous seams. Take the needle through the seam allowances as shown, so that you are only ever stitching through two layers.

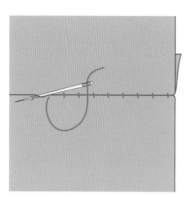

SLIPSTITCH

Slipstitch is good for appliqué or binding, where an invisible finish is required. Make a stitch in the upper fabric from right to left and, as you bring out the needle, catch a couple of threads from the lower fabric. Repeat.

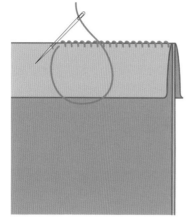

WHIPSTITCH

Whipstitch is used to fasten two edges together. Working from back to front, take tiny stitches at an angle, picking up a few threads from each layer of fabric.

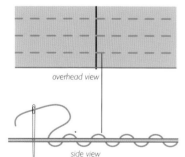

overhead view

side view

STAB STITCH

Use stab stitch instead of running stitch on thick fabrics or multiple layers. Make one stitch at a time through all layers, holding the needle vertically.

Machine stitching

Tip You can keep the stitched patches joined on their thread when you take them to be pressed.

Machine piecing is easy to learn, and once you've mastered chain piecing, your projects will progress much faster. With chain piecing, you stitch pairs of patches one after another without cutting the threads in between.

There's no need to mark the seam allowance on the cut patches. On some sewing machines, a stitching guide on the throat plate is marked with a ¼in (6mm) seam allowance, and sometimes the foot itself is ¼in (6mm) wide, but you can mark the allowance with masking tape or use a foot sold specially for quilters. Use a size 80 needle and cotton thread in a dull color that will blend with the patchwork.

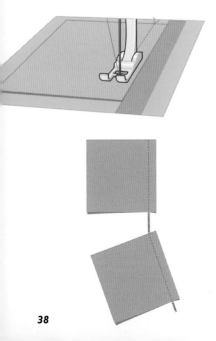

1 Set the stitch length to 10–12 stitches per inch (2.5cm). Use the marks on the machine's throat plate to judge the seam allowance, or measure ¼in (6mm) from the needle and stick down a strip of masking tape.

2 If you are sewing individual patches, start and finish with a few reverse stitches. For chain piecing, stitch the first patch, make a couple of stitches, then feed in the next patch, without cutting the threads.

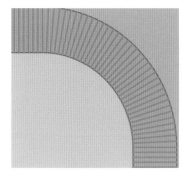

SATIN STITCH
FOR APPLIQUÉ WORK

For machine appliqué, work a close zigzag stitch. Use an embroidery foot and test on some scrap fabric, setting the machine to zigzag, then reducing the stitch length until the stitches are side by side.

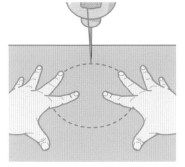

FREEFORM QUILTING

Remove the machine foot, lower the foot lever, and drop the feed dogs if possible. Keep the fabric stretched with your hands, and use them to guide the work.

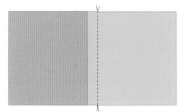

3 Cut the pieces apart and press the seams toward the darker fabric.

4 When joining rows, press the seam allowances in alternate directions to reduce the bulk.

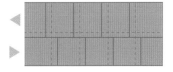

Joining pieces

To join patchwork made from squares, join the squares together in rows, then join the rows to form a block. For blocks with more complicated pieces, join the smaller pieces to form larger ones, then join the larger ones together. Wherever possible, continue to work in rows.

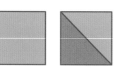
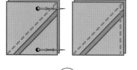

1 Join small triangles to form squares, then join pieced squares to plain squares. The stitched point of the triangle should fall exactly on the seam allowance, ¼in (6mm) from the raw edge.

closeup view

2 Join rows to form a block. Match seams accurately, pin them using pins set at right angles to the seam line, then stitch.

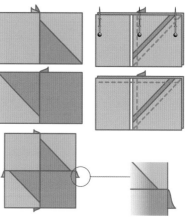

closeup view

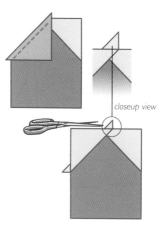

3 Join odd-shaped pieces to form a regular rectangle or square. To join triangles to a pentagon shape, stitch the diagonal seam first, then press and clip off the tails. Join the second triangle, then press and clip off the tails.

closeup view

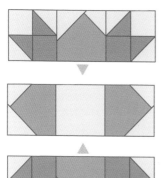

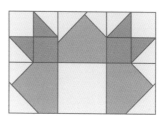

4 Join the small pieced blocks to form rows, then join the rows, matching the seams carefully.

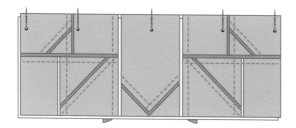

5 To piece angled shapes, instead of aligning the cut edges, make sure the stitching lines match at each end.

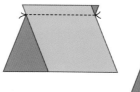

Eight-seam join

When seams meet at one central point, the piecing needs to be very accurate. Take your time, matching the pieces carefully and stitching with exact seam allowances, and you'll get perfect results.

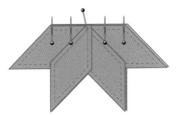

The finished star

1 Join the pieces in pairs along one edge, pinning them with right sides together, then stitching from one corner to the other.

2 Stitch one pair to another pair, pinning and stitching as in step 1. Clip off the tails at the center. Repeat to make the other side of the block.

3 Place the pieces with right sides together and insert a pin through the center of the seam line of one piece, and into the center of the seam line of the other piece. Place more pins as shown. Stitch.

4 If you are hand sewing, fold all the seams in one direction and "spiral," or fan out, the seam allowances at the center; press. If you are machine sewing, press the seam allowances flat as in step 2, then press the final seam in one direction.

Setting in a patch

Not all patchwork seams are stitched in a straight line. Knowing how to set one patch to fit within a right-angled corner and make a neat join is a useful skill.

1 Stitch along the seam line at the inner angle, then use sharp scissors to clip into the point as far as the seam line.

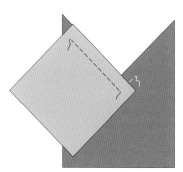

2 Pin the patches together along one straight edge, with right sides together. Stitch the seam, stopping at the staystitched point.

3 Leave the needle in place at the point, and pivot the work to stitch the remaining side, matching the raw edges once again.

4 Press the seam allowance away from the patch so that it lies flat.

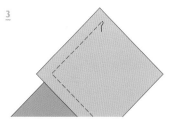

Speed piecing

Making up strips and piecing them together, rather than cutting individual squares, is a speedy, contemporary quiltmaking technique. It relies on a rotary cutter and a sewing machine for quick, accurate results. Cut strips to the desired width, adding ¼in (6mm) seam allowance to each side.

Tip As you join strips, keep checking they are straight, or they'll be unusable. If the strip curves, you may be pulling the top strip when stitching.

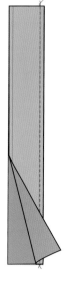

1 Use a rotary cutter and a ruler to cut strips across the full width of the fabric. Stitch a pair of strips together along one long edge, taking a ¼in (6mm) seam. Use a shorter stitch than usual, so that when the units are cut from the strip, the seams do not pull apart. Press the seam allowance to one side.

2 Add further strips to the first pair in the same way, working in the same direction.

Nine-patch blocks

A strip-piecing technique is the simplest way to create a useful nine-patch block, made up of nine equal squares in two colors. In traditional patchwork, each square would be individually stitched to its neighbor, but strip piecing constructs the block in sections, so it's much quicker.

Tip You can cut the strips to any width, but remember to add ¼in (6mm) seam allowances.

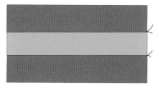
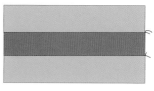

1 Cut 3½in (7.5cm) strips from two contrasting colors. Use the strip-piecing technique on page 44 to join them into two strip-pieced units, each made up of three strips, alternating the colors as shown, so that one unit contains two darker strips and the other unit has two lighter strips.

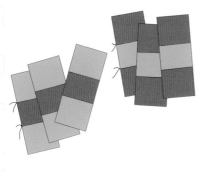

2 Use a rotary cutter and a ruler to cut the strips units into 3½in (7.5cm) pieces.

3 Stitch the three units together, alternating the colors, to form the block.

Half-square triangles

Second only to squares in versatility, half-square triangles are made by cutting a square in half diagonally. You can cut individual triangles, or quick-piece them to make half-square triangle units, as shown here.

1 Decide on the finished unit size and add ⅞in (2.5cm). Cut squares this size from two contrasting fabrics, then mark a diagonal line on the wrong side of the light square.

2 Place the squares with right sides together. Sew a ¼in (6mm) seam on either side of the marked line.

3 Cut along the marked line through both layers. Open out the units and trim to the correct size if necessary.

QUARTER-SQUARE TRIANGLES

Quarter-square triangle units can be made from half-square triangle units. Decide on the finished size of the unit and add 1¼in (3.5cm). Stitch to make half-triangle units, as above. Then place the units with right sides together, matching each dark section to a light one. Follow steps 2 and 3 above to create the quarter-square triangles.

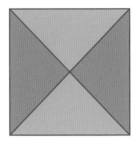

Pressing

Press your work at every stage, lifting and placing the iron, rather than moving it across the fabric. To make seams stronger, press allowances to one side, rather than open. Press toward the darker fabric, so that the allowances do not show on the right side.

Tip If you are pressing the right side of the work, avoid causing shine on the surface by using a press cloth of scrap cotton between the work and the iron.

Set the iron to the correct temperature and place it down flat on the stitched pieces, with right sides together. This sets the seam, flattening out any puckers. Now open out the pieces and place them face down, with the seam allowance to one side. Press gently. Be careful not to distort or stretch the fabric. Turn the fabric right-side up and press again.

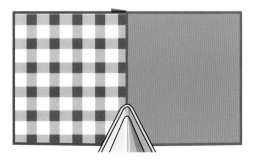

FINGER PRESSING

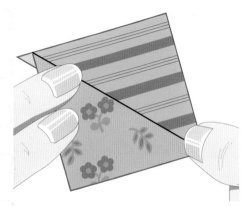

On small patches, or when working with tight angles, it may be easier to use a finger to press the work. Place the stitched piece on a hard surface, right-side up, and run your thumbnail along the seam. You could also use a bought finger-pressing tool for this purpose.

Pressing a four-seam join

At points where two or more seams meet, the seam allowances are annoyingly bulky. Pressing them correctly will help.

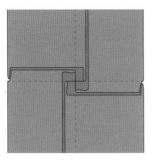

HAND PIECING

At the junction where seams meet, fold each allowance in turn in the same direction, working either clockwise or counterclockwise. Press, first on the wrong side, then on the right side.

MACHINE PIECING

Stitch one seam at a time, each time pressing the seam allowances to one side. To reduce the bulk, press the seams in opposite directions.

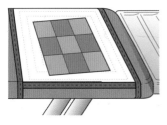

BLOCKING

A patchwork block that is not fully square can be corrected by blocking it. Bind the edges of a 16in (40cm) square of firm fabric, leaving long ends at each corner as ties. Mark the fabric with squares of varying sizes. Tie the mat to the ironing board, then pin the block to it, right-side down, using the mat markings to adjust it so that it is square. Place a damp cloth on top and press.

TRADITIONAL PATCHWORK

TRADITIONAL PATCHWORK

Much of the patchwork we know and love is done

by piecing together fabric shapes to form a block,

then piecing the blocks together to create a quilt.

Another traditional form is the log cabin, which is

made by stitching strips around a central square to

form a block. You can learn these techniques, and

a few popular variations, on the following pages.

Practice by piecing single blocks—they make

great cushion covers.

Building blocks

The simplest patchwork is created from one shape, repeated over and again. But once you start to mix squares, triangles, and other shapes together, there is a wealth of patterns and designs to explore.

ONE-PATCH BLOCKS

These designs are made of just one piece, repeated over and over again. However, don't imagine they're dull, because the way in which the colors are combined can form many patterns, including three-dimensional designs.

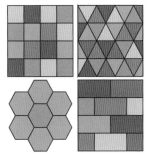

TWO-PATCH BLOCKS

These consist of two shapes. The smaller shape fills in the gaps between the large ones. It's a good idea to make the smaller pieces one color, so that the large shapes stand out from the background.

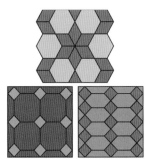

FOUR-PATCH BLOCKS

Much traditional patchwork is based on the four-patch block, and many different patterns can be created from it. However complex the design, it's always divisible into four segments.

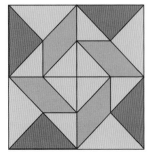

four-patch block	**five-patch block**
block divisible by 4	*block consisting of 25 squares*

seven-patch block	**nine-patch block**
block consisting of 49 squares	*block consisting of 9 squares*

FIVE-PATCH BLOCKS

These blocks consist of 25 squares. Sometimes the finished block is made up of larger patches, but you can always place a five-patch grid over the block and see the divisions.

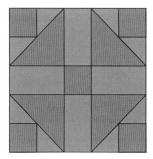

SEVEN-PATCH BLOCKS

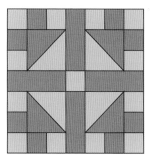

Blocks made up of 49 squares are less common than the other types, but easily make up into designs featuring a central cross.

NINE-PATCH BLOCKS

These have nine squares, and are just as common as four-patch blocks. Nine-patch blocks can be strip-pieced.

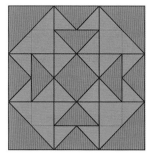

Constructing a four-patch windmill

This simple four-patch block is made up of triangles. It's a good way for beginners to learn to piece a block and practice stitching seams accurately, so that the points of the triangles meet neatly at the center point. You can make this block any size you like. Draw out a right-angled triangle on graph paper, or use the template on page 27. Don't forget to add a ¼in (6mm) seam allowance to all edges.

Tip When stitching the triangles together make sure the seam allowance is a precise ¼in (6mm), then press and measure the patch to check that it is completely square.

Cut four right-angled triangle pieces from plain fabric and four from patterned fabric, including a ¼in (6mm) seam allowance. Make sure the grain of the fabric is aligned with the straight vertical edge of the triangle.

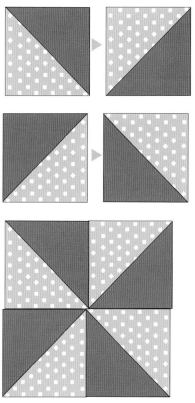

2 With right sides together, join each plain triangle to a patterned one along the diagonal edge, taking a ¼in (6mm) seam. Press the seam allowance toward the darker fabric. Trim off the excess fabric at the corners.

3 Place a pair of patches together, turning them so that the colors alternate. Pin and then stitch them together along one edge. Repeat for the remaining pair of patches. Pin the stitched sections together to form a block. Place a pin through the center seam to make sure that the points match at the center. Stitch a ¼in (6mm) seam. Press the seams toward the darker fabric.

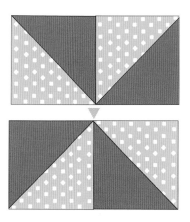

DERWENT • GRAPHIC
ENGLAND

Constructing a nine-patch Texas star

The simplest nine-patch block, made just from squares, can be strip-pieced. However, for this popular design quarter triangles are used, so the block must be pieced in the usual way.

1 Use the block design on page 51 and graph paper to draw out the square and triangle that form the design, adding a seam allowance of ¼in (6mm) to each piece. Cut four squares and four quarter triangles from light-patterned fabric, and a central square from dark-patterned fabric. Choose two plain fabrics and cut four quarter triangles from the lighter one, and eight from the darker one.

2 Stitch the quarter triangles in pairs to form larger triangles, then join the triangles in pairs to form squares. Follow the diagram to get the colors in the correct order. Press the seams to one side.

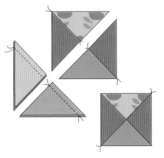

3 Join the patches in rows, following the diagrams, then stitch the rows together to form the finished block. Press the seam allowances to one side.

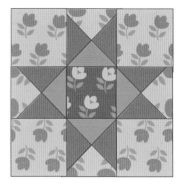

Constructing a five-patch fruit basket

This well known fruit-basket design is based on a five-patch block (see *page 51*), and is a useful lesson in joining patches in sections before stitching the block together.

see *page 51*

Tip Always join the smallest pieces first, such as triangles to form squares, then join the squares into rows of larger blocks.

1 Use the diagram shown in step 4 to draw out on paper the shapes for the block to your required size, excluding the seam allowances shown at the edges of the block. Now add a seam allowance of ¼in (6mm) to each piece. Cut out the shapes from the fabric.

2 Stitch the small triangles together in pairs to make seven half-square triangle units. Join the large triangles in the same way. Stitch a small triangle to one end of each long rectangle.

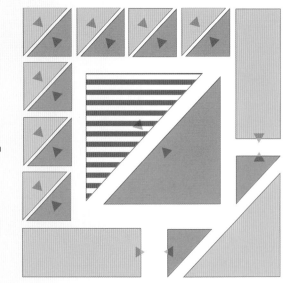

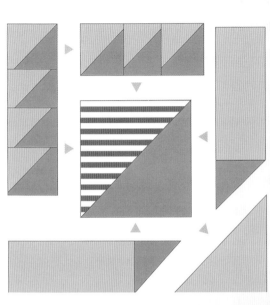

3 Stitch four small half-square triangle units together for the left vertical row, and three units together to form the top horizontal row. Join the horizontal row to the top of the large half-square triangle unit. Join the vertical row to the left side of the large unit.

4 Stitch the rectangle and triangle units to the right-hand edge and bottom, then stitch the large triangle to the corner to complete the block.

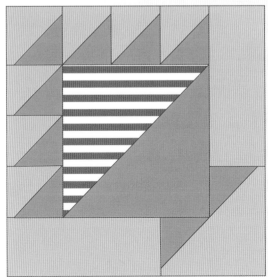

Four-patch blocks

Using graph paper and a pencil (or a photocopier), you can copy or adapt any of these designs to make your own blocks.

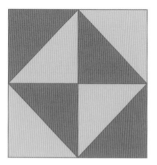

BROKEN DISHES

Simply alternating two colors and using one triangle shape makes a block that has the immediacy and boldness of a flag.

SAWTOOTH

Small repetitive designs like this have a regular rhythm that is very effective. You can make it using the half-square triangle method on page 46.

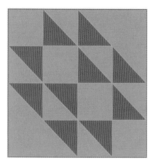

HOVERING HAWKS

These bands of dark triangles appear to hover and float across the background block, particularly when the fabrics are contrasting.

Five-patch blocks

Tip Remember to add a 1/4in (6mm) seam allowance to all pieces.

CROSS AND STAR

Five-patch blocks like these are easily recognizable from their central square, used here as the basis of a cross.

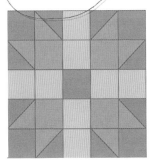

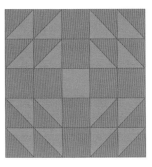

FLYING GEESE FIVE-PATCH

In a five-patch arrangement the triangles seen in sawtooth (*far left*) are turned around to point toward a central square.

SQUARES ON POINT

Four squares on point fill the corners, surrounding a central cross in this pleasing arrangement.

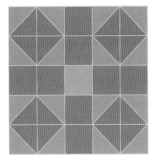

Seven-patch blocks

Because seven-patch blocks are made up of 49 individual squares, very complex designs can be built up, often with a central square and cross design.

BEAR'S TRACKS

This well known block features square patches surrounded by the familiar sawtooth triangles, to create a bear's paw.

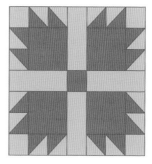

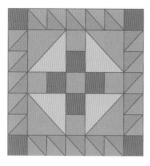

FANCY SET

You can see the similarities with bear's tracks (*above*), but this block introduces extra colors and a square on point.

CALIFORNIA SEVEN

Stars, squares, and triangles all have equal footing in this complicated design, which makes the most of its 49 patches.

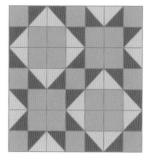

Nine-patch blocks

In its simplest form, a nine-patch block can be strip pieced, but there are plenty more complicated designs to play with and adapt.

PENNSYLVANIA

A change in scale from small to large squares makes for a lively pattern. Add extra colors for interest.

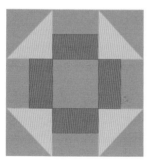

CHURN DASH

The much loved churn dash combines triangles and rectangles for a motif that is quick to stitch, yet appears complex.

HOUSE OF CARDS

In the right colors this motif would have plenty of impact, with its focus on the central diamond.

Stars

One of the prettiest motifs available to quilters, stars have been developed endlessly, from the simplest shapes to the most intricate patterns.

SIMPLE STAR

A recognizable star emerges from basic shapes—namely a central square that is surrounded by triangles around the edges.

RIBBON STAR

This star has a square on point at its center, giving it a more delicate appearance than the simple star above.

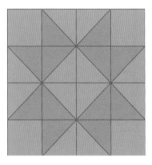

LE MOYNE STAR

This well-known star is a favorite with quilters, thanks to its bold design and sharp points.

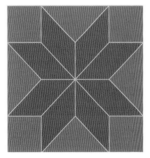

REPEATING STAR

A light star set within a larger dark star calls for careful piecing, but results in a block with plenty of interest.

TEXAS STAR

This deceptively simple star introduces patches made from quarter-square triangles (see page 46). Bring out the shapes by choosing contrasting colors.

VIRGINIA STAR

Although this appears to be a complex mosaic of color, the Virginia Star is simply made up of one repeating shape.

Pictures

Patchwork can be used to create pictures of flowers, animals, baskets, houses, and more. Make sure the ones you choose are instantly recognizable.

SCHOOLHOUSE

The schoolhouse can easily be adapted by altering the blocks forming the windows, doors, and chimney, to make many variations.

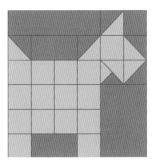

SCOTTIE DOG

This little dog is often spotted on a child's quilt, and he's quite simple to piece from squares and triangles.

FRUIT BASKET

Some variations of this popular fruit-basket design feature a smaller basket with a stitched handle, which is appliquéd after piecing.

Curves

So much patchwork relies on squares that it's good to add the variety of curved pieces into your designs, so that you can expand your repertoire.

SNOWY WINDOWS

The snow hangs from the corner of the windows, creating a very pretty patch that can be repeated or used just at the corners of a quilt.

CABLE ROWS

Every patch in this design is constructed from the same two pieces, and yet they can be arranged to produce a much larger pattern.

MARINER'S COMPASS

A circular motif has a "wow" factor that makes for a wonderful centerpiece for a quilt or a wall hanging.

Amish designs

The shapes of these quilts rely on the "plainness" upheld by Amish folk, but the strong colors and fine quilting make them dramatic. Draft the shapes on graph paper to any size.

DIAMOND IN SQUARE

This traditional pattern is one of the best-known Amish designs. An elaborate medallion was often quilted within the center panel.

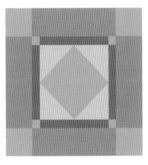

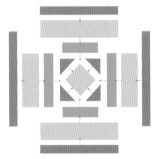

ORDER OF PIECING

Amish designs are quick to piece, because they are made from large sections. Piece together the quilt working from the center outward.

DIAMOND VARIATION

Here, little squares decorate the corners. Other diamond-in-square variations have a pieced central panel, or borders with sawtooth motifs.

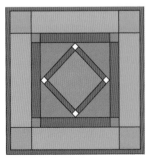

PLAIN QUILT

The pure simplicity of this design, originally from Ohio, leaves lots of scope for involved quilting patterns.

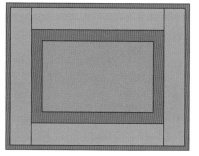

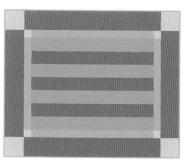

BARS QUILT

Based on a classic early Amish design, the bars of this quilt are also found in "strippy" quilts that originate in the north of England.

SUNSHINE AND SHADOW

Choose a good mix of glowing colors to counteract the darker shades in this jewel-like quilt, which employs a thrifty use of scrap fabrics.

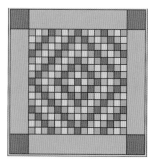

Strip set 1

Constructing double Irish chain

When it's put together this design looks complicated, but if you use the strip-piecing method on page 44, it's easy to achieve.

Strip set 2

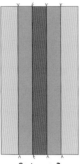

Strip set 3

1 Using light, medium, and dark fabrics, cut 2in (5cm) wide strips across the width of the fabric. Make them up into three sets of strips (see page 44), each containing five strips, matching the colors and shading to the diagram.

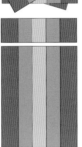

2 Use a rotary cutter and a quilter's ruler to cut each of the strip sets into 2in (5cm) pieces. Make sure that each piece is cut square and accurately. Now you have segments, each containing five patches.

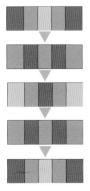

3 Stitch the pieces together in the order shown in the diagram, to form a block. Notice how the darker fabric forms a diagonal cross running from one corner to another.

4 To make the second block, put together and stitch two new strip sets. Strip set 1 has a 5in (12.5cm) light strip surrounded by two darker 2in (5cm) strips. Strip set 2 has a 5in (12.5cm) light strip surrounded by two matching light 2in (5cm) strips.

5 Use a rotary cutter and a ruler to cut Strip set 1 into 2in (5cm) pieces. Then cut Strip set 2 into 5in (12.5cm) pieces.

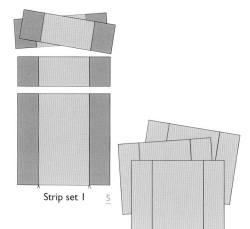

Strip set 1   5

Strip set 2

6 Take a piece from Strip set 2, and join a piece from Strip set 1 on either side of it, forming a block.

7 Stitch alternate blocks together to create the double Irish chain pattern.

Constructing log cabin

Tip Log cabin designs can be made with a hexagon, triangle, or diamond at the center.

Stitching strips around a central block couldn't be easier, yet the interplay of light and dark within the blocks makes for graphic patterns, and the blocks combine to create new patterns. To make complex designs, the center square can be offset or turned on point (that is, rotated so that it stands on its corner, see page 43).

1 Use a rotary cutter and a ruler to cut 2½in (6cm) strips across the width of the fabric in two contrasting colors. Cut a 2½in (6cm) square for the center in a third color.

2 With right sides together, sew a light strip along one side of the center square, taking a ¼in (6mm) seam allowance. Trim the excess strip so that its end matches the edge of the square, and press the seam away from the center square.

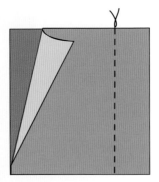

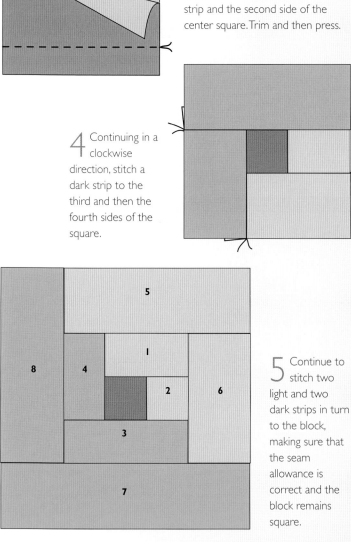

3 Sew a second light strip across the trimmed end of the first strip and the second side of the center square. Trim and then press.

4 Continuing in a clockwise direction, stitch a dark strip to the third and then the fourth sides of the square.

5 Continue to stitch two light and two dark strips in turn to the block, making sure that the seam allowance is correct and the block remains square.

Chain piecing log cabin

Employ this method to make several log cabin blocks at once. Use a rotary cutter and a ruler to cut fabric strips and squares, as on page 68, step 1.

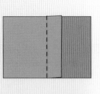

1 With right sides together, pin several center squares along a light strip, with small gaps between them. Stitch the square to the strip along the right edge, taking a ¼in (6mm) seam. Press the seams away from the center square. Cut the pieces apart, trimming away the excess fabric to match the size of the center square.

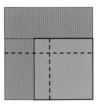

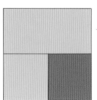

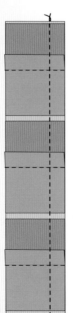

2 With right sides together, pin the square-and-strip pieces to a second light strip, with the center squares at the bottom. Stitch, press, and trim as before.

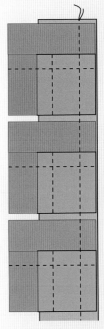

Tip Log cabin designs are quick to make because they don't need sashing or a border.

3 Turn the pieces counterclockwise and stitch them to a dark strip. Press and trim. Repeat to add a fourth (dark) strip.

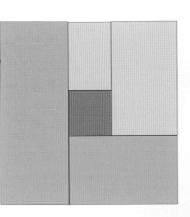

4 Continue adding pairs of light and dark strips until your block is the desired size.

Log cabin designs

Turning the blocks around so that the light- and dark-colored patches are on different sides gives rise to a variety of patterns, all of which are made from the same basic block.

STARRY NIGHT

Arrange four blocks with the darker areas together in the center to form a diamond shape.

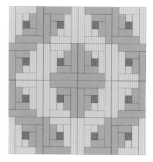

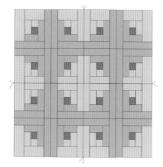

BARN RAISING

Stitch sets of four blocks together with the dark sides meeting in the center, then join these large blocks together to form a four-diamond pattern.

STRAIGHT FURROWS

Alternate the blocks in this design to form a diagonal stepped design across the quilt, resembling furrows in a field.

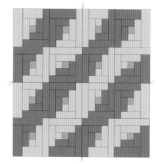

Constructing courthouse steps

This pattern copies the log cabin technique, but adds the strips to the block in a different order, creating a symmetrical block.

1 Take two contrasting fabrics and cut 1½in (4cm) wide strips across them. Cut a 1½in (4cm) center square from a third fabric. With right sides together, sew a light strip to the top of the square. Trim off the excess fabric; press the seam allowance away from the square. Sew a further light strip to the bottom of the square. Trim and press.

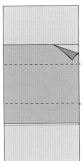

2 Sew a third and fourth strip to each side of the block. Trim and press each seam away from the center square.

3 Continue adding pairs of light and dark strips until the desired size is reached. Keep checking the seam allowances and ensuring that the block is square as you work.

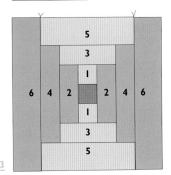

4 Stitch the blocks together in rows, then join the rows to form the quilt.

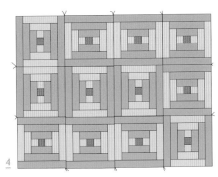

Constructing rail fence

Strip piecing is a fast way to create a lively, colorful design that is perfect for the front of a cushion. See page 44 for a reminder of the basic strip-piecing technique.

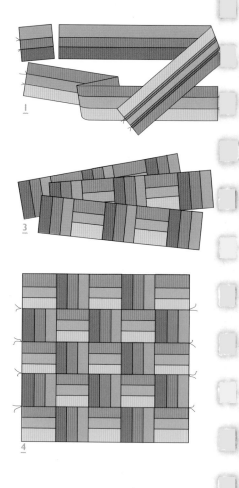

I Take three pale orange and three dark orange fabrics and rotary cut two 1¾in (4.4cm) strips across the width of each. Stitch the three pale fabrics together to form a band, taking a ¼in (6mm) seam allowance. Press the seam allowances open. Repeat, using the darker fabrics.

2 Use a set square and a rotary cutter to cut the strip sets into 4¼in (10.8cm) squares. Cut 13 pale and 12 dark orange segments.

3 Assemble a row of two dark and three pale segments, alternating the shades. Stitch together and press. Now make a row of three dark and two pale segments. Continue, alternating the shades in each row.

4 Join the rows together, alternating the shades, to form the finished block.

FURTHER PIECING
TECHNIQUES

FURTHER PIECING
TECHNIQUES

From English paper piecing to dealing with curved shapes,

folded designs, and crazy patchwork, the variety of piecing

techniques available will satisfy even the most inventive

patchworker. The techniques are not difficult

to learn. Some—like the cathedral window (*see pages*

92–97)—appear complex, yet involve an ingenious

but simple technique. Others—such as foundation

piecing (*see pages 78–79*)—offer a fast and precise

way to stitch accurate seams.

Foundation piecing

Foundation piecing, which is made without templates, is quick and easy. Fabrics are stitched to a background of cotton, nonwoven interfacing, or freezer paper along marked seam lines, eliminating the need for perfect cutting and precise seam allowances.

Before you start piecing the fabric, work out the logical order for stitching the patches. Sometimes it's best to work from the center outward; for other designs, it may be better to work from side to side. For intricate designs it's often best to stitch some patches together before joining them to the foundation.

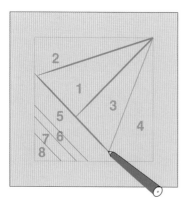

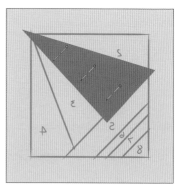

1 Trace the patchwork design in reverse onto the foundation fabric, interfacing, or freezer paper. Make sure the foundation is large enough to allow a good margin all around the design. Number the pieces in a logical order for piecing.

2 Cut out patch 1, making it at least ¼in (6mm) larger than the traced outline on all sides. Pin it right side up to the unmarked side of the foundation.

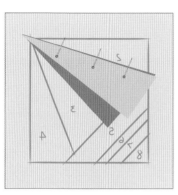

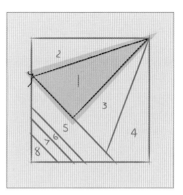

3 Cut out the second patch, at least ¼in (6mm) larger all around, as before. Pin this patch to the first patch, with right sides together.

4 Turn over and stitch the marked seam between patch 1 and patch 2, along the seam line. Trim the seam allowance to ¼in (6mm) from the seam line.

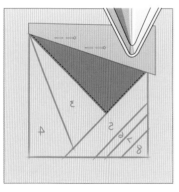

5 Turn the work over again, flip patch 2 open, and press.

6 Stitch patch 3 in the same manner, then continue stitching patches. Make sure the fabric patches overlap the edge of the design by at least ¼in (6mm). If you are using freezer paper, tear it away when the design is complete.

String patchwork

The perfect way of using up all those narrow strips from piecing or dressmaking projects, string patchwork makes lively, striped panels that can be cut into all sorts of shapes.

Tip Wash strings before making them up, placing them in a mesh bag to prevent fraying.

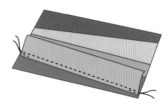

1 | Choose fabric pieces of similar length and in varied colors and patterns. The more contrast there is between the colors, the better. Stitch these "strings" together, taking ¼in (6mm) seams.

2 By shifting the position of the string you are adding, you can create angled pieces. Press all the seam allowances to one side.

Strings on a base

This method of patchwork works by stitching strings to a patch cut from foundation fabric. It's a good way of using up leftover strings that are too short for a larger project.

1 | Cut a foundation piece from freezer paper or fabric, allowing a ¼in (6mm) seam allowance. Position the first string on the right side of the foundation, in the center and right side upward. Cut off the spare fabric, close to the foundation.

2 Place the second string over the first, right sides together. Stitch through all layers, close to the lower edge of the strings. Flip open the strings and press.

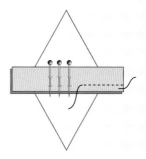

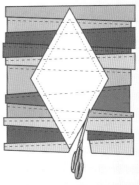

3 Turn the template so that the first string is at the bottom, and add a third string as before. Keep adding strings until the foundation is completely covered.

4 Turn to the wrong side and cut carefully around the edge of the foundation. If you are using a paper foundation, tear it away.

5 Use the string patchwork and strings on a base piece to make up borders, stars, or other patterns.

English piecing

Tip You can buy templates for hexagons, triangles, and diamonds, or work out the designs on isometric paper. You could also use octagons, but you need to intersperse them with squares; 12 pentagons stitched together make a ball shape.

This favorite old method of piecing uses paper patterns, each patch being stitched to a paper. The whole quilt is made up before the papers are removed. It is a hand-sewing technique, so it's easy to carry a bag of pieces around with you and stitch small amounts at a time.

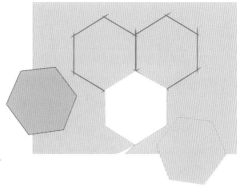

1 Trace the hexagon template on page 26 (or use a ready-made template), then draw around it on freezer paper, drawing enough shapes to complete your project. Cut out the shapes carefully.

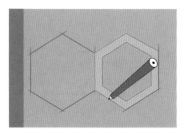

2 Press the papers onto the wrong side of the fabric, leaving gaps between them so that you can mark a ¼in (6mm) seam allowance around each piece.

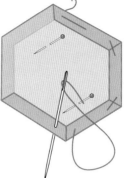

3 Fold the edge of the fabric over the edge of the freezer paper template and baste, starting with a knot on the right side. Continue folding and basting each edge in turn.

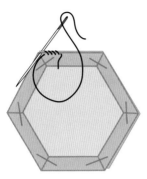

4 Place two patches with right sides together. Starting ¼in (6mm) from the left edge, take tiny neat stitches through both layers from back to front, picking up just a few threads of fabric with each stitch and working toward the left corner. Do not pierce the freezer papers.

5 Stitch from the left corner to the right one, covering the previous stitches. Keep the stitches fairly loose so that the seam will lie flat. Do not pierce the paper. To fasten off, work a few stitches from right to left, over the previous stitching.

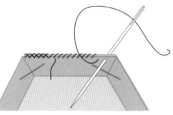

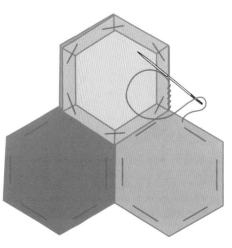

6 Continue adding patches, using the same thread where possible. When the work is complete, remove the basting and the papers, then press.

Hexagon patterns

Simple hexagon shapes can form exciting patterns across your quilt, if you select your colors and prints carefully.

GRANDMOTHER'S FLOWER GARDEN

Choose a strong color for the flower center and a contrasting color for the petals.

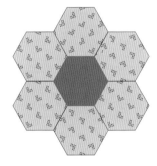

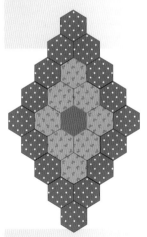

FIELD OF DIAMONDS

Make the grandmother's flower garden patch shown above, then add an extra hexagon to the top and bottom. Add further rows to make larger diamonds.

OCEAN WAVE

This useful wave motif makes a great border for a quilt made of hexagons.

Diamond patterns

Pieced diamonds can have a 3D effect if you select the fabric tones with care. Make sure the points are accurate so that the diamonds look crisp. Diamonds also work well with triangles and hexagons.

INNER CITY

Blocks of nine diamonds form this three-dimensional shape. Choose light and dark shades with care, to get the maximum effect.

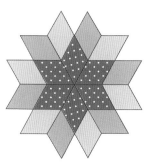

SIX-POINT STARS

Join six diamonds to form a star, then add further diamonds as desired to increase the size.

BRICK PILE

Use a pair of diamonds side by side to make up the "tops" of the bricks.

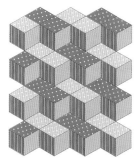

Curved patchwork

Piecing curves is easier than you might think, and adds a whole new dimension to your patchworking. It's easiest to do by hand, although you can also use a sewing machine.

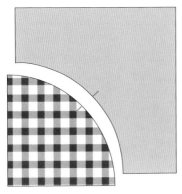

1 Use the drunkard's path templates on page 31 (or draft your own pattern) to cut the two shapes from contrasting fabrics, matching the straight grain to the straight edges of the pieces. Fold the shapes in half along the curved edge, and press with a finger to mark the center.

2 With right sides together and the concave shape on top, pin the straight edges and the center points together. Arrange pins along the raw edges between these two points, fitting the convex and concave curves together. Pin the remaining half of the curve in the same way.

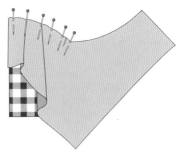

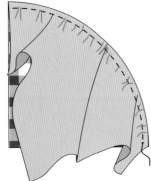

3 Stitch a ¼in (6mm) seam by hand. Alternatively, work by machine, easing out the pins as you go. Press the seam allowance toward the concave section. Check that the patch is square.

Drunkard's path

Use the curved patches on page 86 to make up a drunkard's path block using 16 patches. Choose contrasting colored fabrics for maximum effect. This graphic design would work well in black and white.

1 Use the templates on page 31 to cut eight convex and concave shapes from light fabric, and the same number from dark fabric. Stitch the pieces to form square patches, as shown on page 86, matching each light concave piece to a dark convex piece, and vice versa.

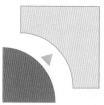

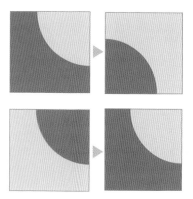

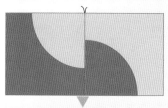

2 Now arrange the patches as shown and stitch them together in pairs.

3 Stitch the pairs of patches together to form a block. Make up four identical blocks, then turn them around to create the design shown on page 88. Stitch the blocks together, pressing the seam allowances to one side.

Tip Try out your designs on graph paper, or make up several patches and play around with them until you get a satisfying result.

Drunkard's path variations

Drunkard's path is an extremely versatile pattern, and very different effects can be obtained by repeating and rotating the blocks.

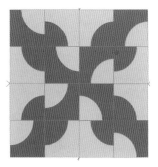

DRUNKARD'S PATH

This is the finished block that is created by following the instructions on page 87.

MILL WHEEL

In this pattern the colors are reversed to make alternate blocks.

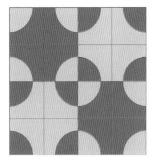

FALLING TREES

This features a wavy line running diagonally through the blocks.

More curved designs

Here are just a few examples of the many designs that are possible once you have mastered curved seams. You can either buy templates for these patterns or make your own. If the design has small pieces, make the patches large, so that you can manipulate the shapes easily.

ORANGE PEEL

This design has a simple but highly effective motif.

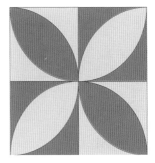

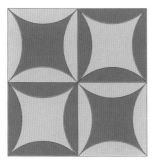

ROBBING PETER TO PAY PAUL

This four-patch block has a "stretched" square design.

TENNESSEE CIRCLE

This bold and dramatic design looks striking in contrasting main colors.

Folded star

Tip Avoid large-scale patterns, which will not show up well when they are folded.

Using folded triangles to create intricate designs results in a thick, layered patchwork that does not need to be quilted. The method is fairly simple and is ideal for small projects such as bags, cushions, and accessories.

1 Cut a square of lightweight foundation fabric the size of the finished block plus a 2in (5cm) margin all round. Cut 2in (5cm) fabric squares as follows: Round 1, four squares; Round 2, eight contrasting squares; Round 3, eight contrasting squares; subsequent rounds, 16 contrasting squares. Fold the small squares in half and press. Make two diagonal folds as shown, bringing the corner points together at the center of the base line. Press.

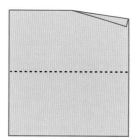

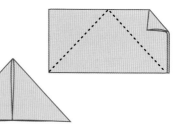

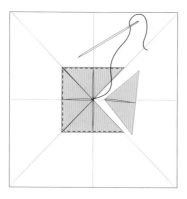

2 Mark the foundation square with horizontal, vertical, and diagonal lines meeting at the center. To make Round 1, pin the first row of four triangles in position, with the points meeting at the center. Slipstitch the points to the foundation fabric. Sew running stitch around the edges to hold them in place.

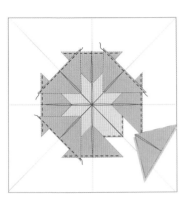

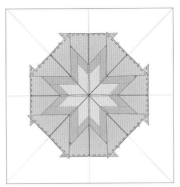

3 For Round 2, stitch four triangles to the top, bottom, and sides of the work, overlapping the first round and with each point ½in (12mm) from the center. Then add four further triangles to the corners, overlapping the ones you have just stitched.

4 Make Round 3 in the same way, adding a triangle to the top, bottom, and sides, then to each of the four corners.

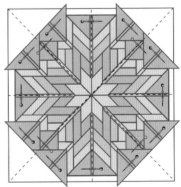

5 Make Round 4 in the same way, pinning eight triangles in place, then adding a further eight to overlap them.

6 Continue making rounds until the gaps are filled. You can add triangles to fill the missing corners to form a square, or trim the edges of the star to make a circle. To use the folded star as an appliqué, bind the raw edges.

Cathedral window

Tip Use a motif fabric for the contrast squares, centering a motif in each "window."

When you look at this puzzling design, it's hard to see how it's constructed. In fact, it's quite simple; the decorative inserts (or windows) are held in place by the rolled and folded edges of the plain fabric, which is made up of folded squares.

TO STITCH BY HAND

1 Cut four 8½in (21.2cm) squares from plain fabric (or choose your own measurements, using the calculation given opposite). Press the raw edges ¼in (6mm) to the wrong side and baste.

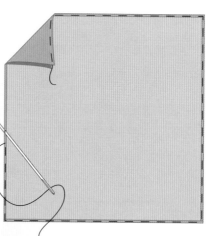

2 Fold the four corners of the fabric square to the center. Press and pin them in place.

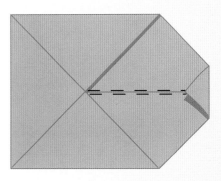

Cathedral window calculation
A finished block (consisting of four folded squares) is about half the size of one of the cut squares. To calculate the size of the cut squares, take the required finished size of your block, multiply by two, and add ½in (12mm).

3 Fold the corners again to the center. Press and pin them in place.

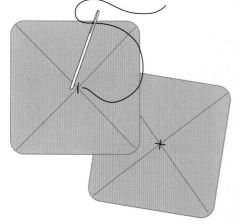

4 At the center, make a cross stitch through all the layers to secure the corners in place. Remove the pins. (Continued overleaf.)

Cathedral window

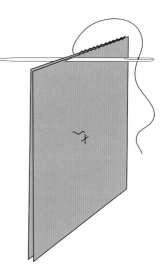

5 With right sides together, oversew two of the squares together along one edge, just catching a few threads with each stitch. Finish the corners securely. Repeat, using the second pair of squares.

6 Oversew the two rows of stitched squares together to form a square.

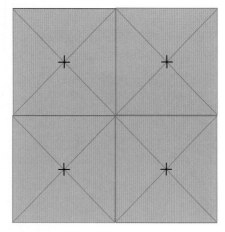

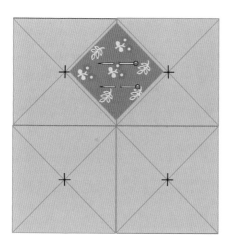

7 Cut four squares of contrast fabric, to fit just inside one "frame" of the foundation fabric. Pin them in place.

8 Roll a folded edge of the plain fabric over the raw edge of the contrast fabric and slipstitch it in place, using thread to match the plain fabric. Repeat to cover the remaining raw edges of the contrast patch. Add further inserts in the same way. Either leave the corners plain or fill them with contrast triangles.

Cathedral window

TO STITCH BY MACHINE

In this speedy method the foundation squares are machine stitched, saving time and effort. If you choose this method you will have to work very accurately to make the corners as sharp as hand-pieced ones. You will still need to secure the contrast "windows" by hand.

Using cathedral window

Cathedral window isn't a true patchwork technique, since it has no backing, batting, or quilting. However, the resultant thick fabric of folded layers is good for small projects, such as a table runner, cushion, bag, or wall hanging.

1 Cut four plain fabric squares (see page 90, step 1). Fold each square in half, right sides together, and stitch the short edges, taking a ¼in (6mm) seam. Trim the corners.

2 Open out the shape, and bring the ends of the seams together to form a pouch. Pin the raw edges together. Stitch the seam from each corner toward the center, but leave a gap at the center. Turn through to the right side, gently easing the corners into place. Slipstitch the opening to finish the seam.

3 Press the square, then fold the corners to the center point and press again to mark a crease.

4 Place two squares with wrong sides together, and open up a corresponding fold from each. Use the pressed crease as a guideline to stitch the two squares together, starting and finishing with backstitches.

5 Join rows of folded squares in the same way, matching the seams carefully. Backstitch at the corners and where the seams meet. Fold the flaps to the center and cross stitch in place (see page 93, step 4). Cut and hand sew inserts (see page 95, steps 7–8).

Shell patchwork

These pretty clamshells, also known as fish scales, are appliquéd to a background fabric.

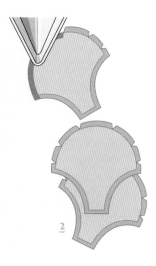

1 Use the template on page 28 to mark and cut several clamshells from freezer paper. Press the templates to the wrong side of the fabric, with the straight grain of the fabric running vertically through each patch. Allow gaps of at least ½in (12mm) around each template.

2 Mark a ¼in (6mm) seam allowance around each piece and cut them out. Clip the seam allowance around the curved edge. Fold the curved edge over the paper and press.

3 Use chalk or basting stitches to mark a horizontal line on the background fabric. Pin the clamshells to this line, right-sides up, with the sides touching. Slipstitch the shells in place along the top edges only. Remove the freezer paper templates.

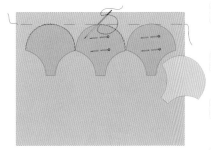

4 Place the next row of patches over the first row and stitch the curved edges. Remove the freezer paper. Repeat to make further rows.

Clamshell patterns

Arranging the clamshells in diagonal rows or groups
of different colors enables you to create repeating
patterns that can be highly effective.

DIAGONAL ROWS

Arrange your colors, or light and
dark fabrics, so that the clamshells
form diagonal rows.

CLAMSHELL GROUPS

Organize the clamshells so that
they form groups of four.

DOUBLE AXEHEAD

You can use a template shaped like
an apple core to make this pattern.
Alternate pieces are then placed
horizontally and vertically to form
the double axeheads.

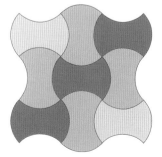

Fans

Make the fan block in the same way as the plate, but use fewer segments, and add a quarter circle at the narrow end.

Dresden plates and fans

These circular plate motifs are great for appliqué projects, while the fans, which are made in the same way, can be set into a block to make a quilt. You can divide up the plate or fan into as many even segments as you wish, and the outer edges can be curved, pointed, or scalloped. Use the template on page 30, cutting fewer or more segments, as desired.

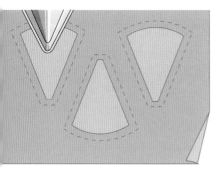

Trace the template on page 30, drawing around the inner line, and cut out the segments and a circle for the center from iron-on interfacing. Press the interfacing patches onto the wrong side of the fabric, allowing ½in (12mm) gaps between them, and making sure that the straight grain of the fabric runs vertically through the segments.

2 Mark a ¼in (6mm) seam allowance around each piece, then cut out the segments and circle. Clip curves at the top of the segments. Clip around the edges of the circle.

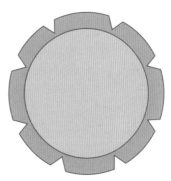

3 With right sides together, stitch a pair of segments along one side, following the edge of the interfacing. Start within the seam allowance at the top, and end at the narrow edge.

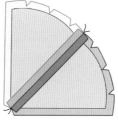

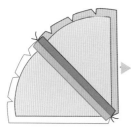

4 Stitch the remaining segments in pairs in the same way. Join the pairs to make a semicircle. Stitch the two semicircles to form the plate.

5 Fold under the seam allowance around the curved outer edges of the plate and baste in place. Sew the plate to a background fabric. Using small stitches, oversew the circle to the center.

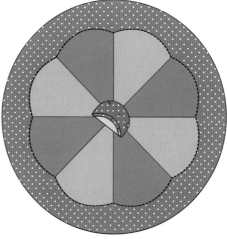

Dresden plate patterns

You can vary both the width of the segments and the shape of the outside edges to make different Dresden plate patterns.

SUNSPLASH

This design uses a combination of points and curved edges.

FLOWER PLATE

Curved segments can be used to create the petals of a flower.

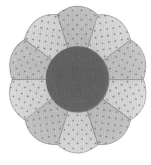

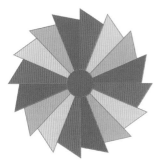

CIRCULAR SAW

Angled edges on the outside form a saw, or windmill, effect.

Fan patterns

If you stitch a quarter-circle fan without the quarter circle at its point, the fan can be set into a block using the curved seam method (see *page 86*). You can then arrange the blocks to create different patterns.

WHEEL

Four fans meeting at a central point create a circle in this wheel design.

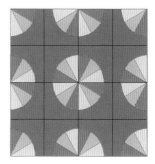

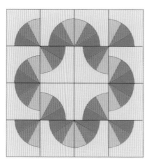

MOHAWK TRAIL

The Mohawk trail uses fans to create a central motif within a block.

FALLING TREES

In this design runs of color snake across the block like falling trees.

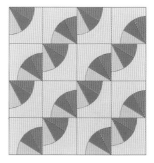

Crazy patchwork

In crazy patchwork random fabrics and shapes are cut and stitched to an unmarked background fabric, resulting in a riot of color and pattern. The secret is to make every patch different.

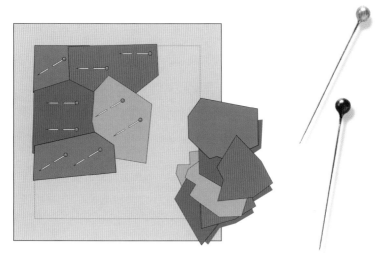

1 Cut a piece of fabric to the size of the finished project, allowing a 1in (2.5cm) border all around. Then cut patches into random shapes and pin them to the foundation, with right sides up and overlapping. Move the patches around until the design looks good, with no foundation showing.

2 To hand stitch, first tuck under and baste the exposed raw edges in the center of the block, but leave those around the perimeter of the block unstitched. Work embroidery stitches such as feather stitch or herringbone stitch (see opposite) across the joins, stitching through all the layers.

   To machine stitch, baste the pieces in place, but leave all the raw edges unturned. Use satin stitch or open zigzag to cover all the joins.

USING IRON-ON INTERFACING

Cut a piece of iron-on interfacing as for the fabric foundation (step 1 *opposite*) and arrange the patches, as before. Set the iron to a temperature to suit the fabric, and press in place. Turn over and press again from the other side.

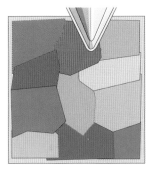

SEW AND FLIP

You can also adapt the foundation piecing method on pages 78–79. Place two patches in the foundation center with right sides together, raw edges matching, and stitch the seam. Flip open the patch, then add a new patch and stitch again.

FEATHER STITCH

Bring the needle out near the edge of the left-hand patch and insert it into the right-hand patch. Take a diagonal stitch through the right patch, looping the loose thread beneath it. Now make a stitch on the left patch in the same way.

HERRINGBONE STITCH

Bring the needle up through the lower fabric and insert it diagonally above and to the right into the upper fabric, taking a small stitch from right to left. Now insert it into the lower fabric, diagonally and to the right, taking a small stitch from right to left.

Seminole

Tip Cut the outer strips of the band wider than the inner ones, because the extra fabric makes the band easier to handle. You can trim off the excess once the band is made up.

Developed by the Seminole people of the Florida Everglades, this distinctive style was made using hand-operated sewing machines from the late 1800s. It consists of horizontal bands of machine-stitched patchwork, usually in brilliant colors. The bands are cut into narrow strips and then put back together in different positions to make the intricate patterns.

You can make the strips as wide or narrow as you choose; just remember to add ¼in (6mm) seam allowances to each side. Using a rotary cutter will speed up the cutting process.

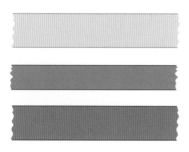

1 Use a rotary cutter and a quilter's ruler to cut strips across the width of your fabrics in contrasting colors. Here two strips 1¾in (4.2cm) wide, and one strip 1¼in (3cm) wide, have been used.

2 Stitch the strips together, taking a ¼in (6mm) seam allowance and sandwiching the narrow strip between the wider ones. Press the seam allowances in one direction. Use the point of the iron to press along the seam lines, but take care not to stretch the fabrics.

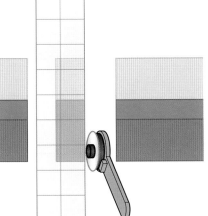

3 Using a rotary cutter and a quilter's ruler, cut 1¼in (3cm) pieces from the strip set, checking that they are exactly square.

4 Place the pieces together as shown, aligning the seams carefully, and stitch together, taking a ¼in (6mm) seam allowance. Press the seam allowances in one direction.

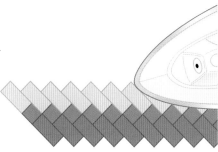

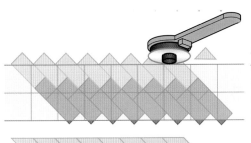

5 Lay a ruler across the top of the band and use it as a guide to trim off the pointed edges with the rotary cutter. Repeat at the bottom of the band.

Seminole variations

Some Seminole variations look so complex that it's hard to believe they are pieced from straightforward strips. Here are some examples of straight, offset, and angled repeats, plus a few other variations.

STRAIGHT REPEATS

Strips are made of two or more colors, cut straight across the strip to make the pieces, then alternate pieces are turned around to form a pattern.

NARROW BANDS

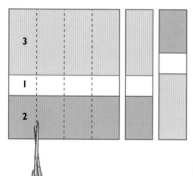

1 Cut strips in a ratio of 3:1:2, as shown. Stitch the strips together, then cut them into pieces.

2 Arrange the pieces as shown, turning alternate pieces around, then stitch them to form a band.

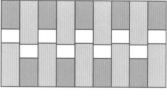

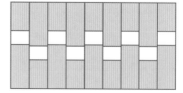

CHECKERBOARD

1 For pattern A, cut and stitch five strips of similar width, then cut them into pieces. For pattern B, cut and stitch three strips in a ratio of 2:1:2, then cut them into pieces.

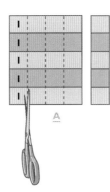

A

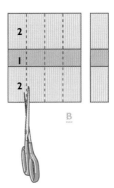

B

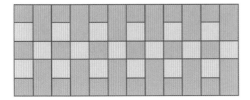

2 Place a pattern A piece next to a pattern B piece, and repeat to make the design, as shown. Stitch the pieces together.

Measuring strips

Instead of giving measurements, the designs are given as ratios. This means that you can make the bands any size you choose. For example, a ratio of 3:1:3 means that the two outer strips are cut three times as wide as the central strip.

OFFSET DESIGNS

To create these designs, the cut pieces are "offset"—that is, each piece is lined up one step down from its neighbor.

OFFSET NARROW BANDS

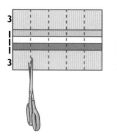

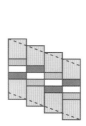

1 Cut five strips in a ration of 3:1:1:1:3, and stitch them together. Then cut them into pieces.

2 Alternate the pieces to form the pattern and offset them, then stitch them together.

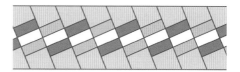

OFFSET PLAIN AND PIECED

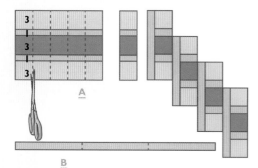

A

B

1 For pattern A, cut strips in a ratio of 3:1:3:1:3 and stitch them together. Then cut them into pieces. For pattern B, cut plain strips, to the same length as the pattern A pieces. Stitch each piece A to a piece B.

2 Match up the pieces as shown and offset them, then stitch them to form the design.

ANGLED REPEATS

Cutting pieces at an angle, instead of straight across, creates slanted strips and diamond patterns.

ANGLED BARS

1 Stitch two contrasting strips together. Then cut the strips into pieces at a 45-degree angle.

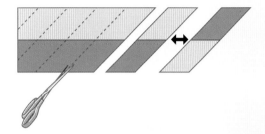

2 Turn alternate pieces around and stitch them together to form the pattern.

FINE DIAMONDS

1 Make up a strip set following the instructions on pages 106–107, steps 1–2. Then cut the strip into pieces at a 45-degree angle.

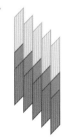

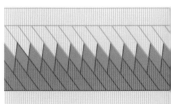

2 Stitch the pieces together to form a band as shown, matching the seam lines carefully.

Seminole blocks

You can use Seminole techniques to quick-piece a block. The method is similar to the strip-piecing techniques shown on pages 44–45, but the blocks can be quite complex.

1 Make pattern A from two strips in a ratio of 2:3. Stitch them together, then cut them apart. Make pattern B from strips in a ratio of 2:1:2. Stitch them together and cut them into pieces.

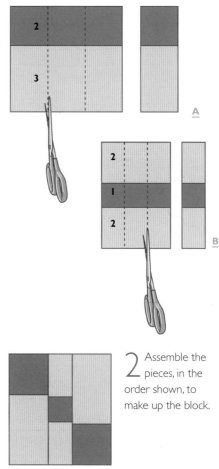

A

B

2 Assemble the pieces, in the order shown, to make up the block.

APPLIQUÉ

APPLIQUÉ

Stitching smaller pieces to a background fabric

for a decorative effect is known as appliqué, and it

can be used alone to make a quilt or combined

with pieced patchwork blocks. Appliqué can be

worked neatly by hand or using machine satin stitch

(see page 121). Look out for pictorial fabric designs

such as flowers, birds, and fruit to cut for

your appliqué projects.

Preparing templates

Whether you choose hand or machine appliqué, the first job is to transfer your design onto the appliqué fabric. Opt for bold designs rather than intricate shapes.

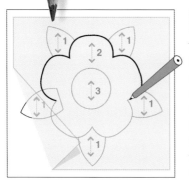

If you are working from a photograph or drawing, make sure the shapes are simple enough to cut out and stitch. If the shapes are complicated, see whether you can simplify the design. For example, details such as flower stems can be embroidered once the appliqué is finished. Trace your design onto tracing paper or freezer paper, numbering the pieces to denote colors or the order in which they will be stitched.

2 Cut out the paper shapes and use them as a pattern for cutting the pieces from the fabric. (Depending on your choice of appliqué method, you may need to add a seam allowance.) Assemble the pieces in the order marked on your tracing, overlapping the shapes if necessary.

Hand appliqué

When stitching appliqué by hand, you have the choice of working small, almost hidden stitches, or making the stitches stand out so that they enhance your design.

RAW-EDGE APPLIQUÉ

You can either work with a non-fraying fabric such as felt, or back fabric pieces with iron-on interfacing (*see below*). Use a paper template (*see opposite*) to cut out the appliqué shape without a seam allowance. Pin and baste the appliqué to the right side of the background fabric, then blind stitch (*see page 118*) the shape in place.

USING IRON-ON INTERFACING

This method produces a sharp edge.

1 Trace a design onto the shiny side of the iron-on interfacing and cut it out. Turn the interfacing over, placing it shiny-side down on the wrong side of the fabric. Press with a steam iron.

2 Mark a ⅜in (9mm) seam allowance around the shape, then cut it out. Press the seam allowance over the interfacing edge and baste in place. Blind stitch the appliqué on the background fabric.

TRADITIONAL APPLIQUÉ

For fabrics that fray, turn under a seam allowance with the point of the needle as you sew, or use this paper template method.

1 Pin the paper template right side down on the wrong side of the appliqué fabric. Mark on a seam allowance of ⅜in (9mm) and cut out.

2 Fold and press the seam allowance over the edges of the paper template. Clip any curved edges, then remove the paper and baste the seam allowance in place. Stitch the appliqué to the background fabric.

FREEZER-PAPER METHOD

For a sharper turning on appliqué edges, use freezer paper.

Trace the template onto the non-shiny side of the freezer paper and cut out. Position the freezer paper shiny-side up on the back of your fabric shape and draw around it, adding a ⅜in (9mm) seam allowance. Cut it out. Use the point of a dry iron to press the seam allowance over the edge of the paper, then blind stitch the shape to the background fabric. On the wrong side, cut away the background fabric and remove the freezer paper.

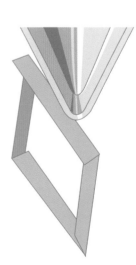

SHAPED PIECES

Curves, corners, and points need special care, so that the shapes will lie flat when they are appliquéd.

CURVES

1 For inner curves, clip the seam allowance to within ⅛in (3mm) of the seam line. Make your clips closer together if the curve is pronounced. Press or baste the seam allowance, ensuring that the clipped edges lie flat.

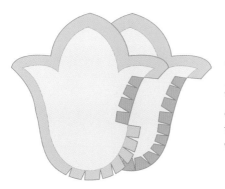

2 For outer curves, clip the seam allowance as above. You can remove small notches of fabric to reduce the bulk so that the appliqué will lie flat when applied to the fabric.

CORNERS AND POINTS

1 On inner corners, clip the seam allowance very close to the seam line. Fold the adjacent seam allowances into position and stitch.

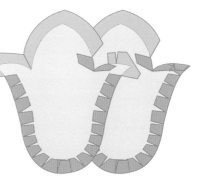

2 On outer corners and other angles, trim the point before folding it, to remove excess bulk. Fold the seam allowance over the point, then fold the two adjacent sides and stitch.

Hand appliqué stitches

Tip With blanket stitch you can either use small stitches for a neat effect, or large ones for a naïve style.

When appliquéing by hand you can either make stitches almost invisible or go for bold, decorative stitches. For some projects it's better to opt for an unobtrusive effect, using blind stitch and matching thread, to hide your stitches as much as possible. For other projects the stitches themselves become an important part of the design. Plain stitches such as running stitch, backstitch, or stab stitch (see page 37) work well. For a fancy effect, try blanket stitch.

BLIND STITCH

Bring the needle out on the right side of the background fabric, next to the edge of your appliqué. Insert the needle into the appliqué, close to the folded edge. Repeat, making stitches ⅛in (3mm) apart.

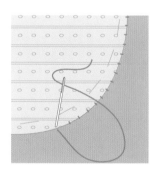

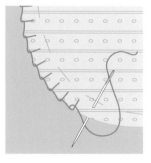

BLANKET STITCH

Bring the needle out on the right side of the background fabric, next to the edge of your appliqué. Insert the needle within the appliqué shape, slightly to the right, and bring it out directly below, tucking the spare thread beneath the needle. Repeat.

Machine appliqué

Stitching appliqué by machine is fast, and you don't have to worry about turning under raw edges, because the stitching will cover them. This method makes durable appliqué that can be washed over and over again without damaging it. Look out for a clear appliqué foot for your sewing machine, so that you can see the stitching edges clearly.

MACHINE STITCH AND CUT
Use a straight stitch for close-woven fabrics that don't fray easily, and satin stitch to protect fabrics that may fray.

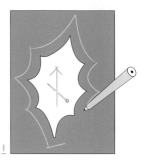

1 Trace the shapes onto freezer paper, shiny-side down. Cut them out. Press the freezer-paper pieces onto the right side of the appliqué fabric and use a marker to draw around them, then draw a seam allowance of at least ½in (12mm) all around and cut them out.

2 Pin the appliqué shape to the background fabric.

3 Machine stitch along the marked line. Trim the fabric close to the stitching with sharp embroidery scissors. If you wish, finish the appliqué by going over the stitched line with satin stitch (see page 121), taking care to cover the raw edges.

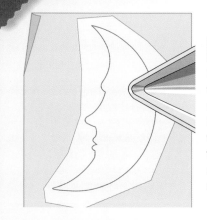

FUSIBLE WEB

Fusible web is ideal for raw-edge appliqué. The web is sandwiched between the appliqué motif and the background fabric, and the heat from the iron sets the adhesive and sticks them together. It's a useful technique for complicated appliqué shapes.

1 Trace the design onto the non-shiny side of freezer paper and cut it out. Place the paper template wrong-side up on the smooth side of the fusible web and draw around it with a marker. Cut out the shape, with a ½in (12mm) margin. With the rough side down, press the shape to the wrong side of the appliqué fabric.

2 Cut out the design carefully along the marked line, using sharp scissors. Peel off the backing paper.

3 Place the appliqué in position on the background fabric and press it to bond it in place. Finish the edges with machine satin stitch (see *opposite*).

120

Machine appliqué stitches

Tip Leave long threads so that you can thread a needle and take the thread to the wrong side of the work by hand.

ZIGZAG AND SATIN STITCH

Practice these stitches on fabric scraps first, adjusting the stitch length and width as necessary. Satin stitch is worked in the same way as zigzag, but the stitches are closer together.

1 Zigzag along the edge of the appliqué. On a tight outer curve, stop with the needle on the right edge of the appliqué. Pivot the fabric, stitch a little further, then stop and pivot again. For an inner curve, stop with the needle on the inside of the curve before you pivot.

2 On outer corners, stop with the needle to the right of the appliqué shape. Leaving the needle in the background fabric, pivot the work and continue stitching.

3 On inner corners, stop with the needle on the left, within the appliqué shape, then pivot the work and continue stitching.

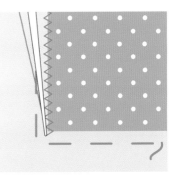

Cut-and-sew appliqué

With this method, the appliqué design is basted to the background fabric before cutting out. Not much basting is needed, and the cutting and stitching are done as you work around the appliqué shape.

1 Make a freezer-paper template of the design and draw around it, or draw a motif freehand on the right side of the appliqué fabric. Position the appliqué fabric on the right side of the background fabric, with straight grain matching. Baste the design to the background, keeping the stitching ¼in (6mm) within the marked lines of the motif.

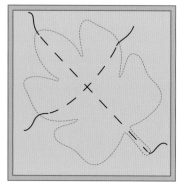

2 Cut away one section of the appliqué fabric, ¼in (6mm) from the marked seam line. Clip any curves close to the seam line.

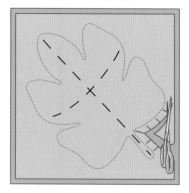

3 Slipstitch the appliqué to the background, turning under the seam allowance with the tip of the needle as you go. Continue cutting and stitching until the appliqué is completed, then remove the basting.

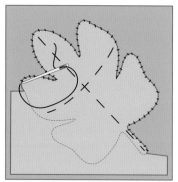

Broderie perse

Cutting printed motifs from a decorative fabric and using them for appliqué is called broderie perse, since it was thought to resemble Persian embroidery. In nineteenth-century America chintz fabrics were specially designed with motifs to use as appliqués.

1 Wash the fabrics and choose your motifs. If a motif has fine details, such as a flower stem, do not cut these because they can be embroidered on later. Cut out the pieces, allowing ¼in (6mm) all around.

2 Clip curves close to the stitching line. You can fold and baste the seam allowance to the wrong side now, or do it while you are stitching the motif.

3 Arrange the motifs on the background fabric and slipstitch to secure it in place. Embroider any missing details.

Hawaiian appliqué

Tip To machine
stitch Hawaiian
appliqué, first
bond the appliqué
fabric to fusible
web (*see page
120*). Mark and
cut out the design
and fuse it to the
background fabric,
then zigzag or
satin stitch over
the raw edges.

Every child knows the fun of cutting snowflakes
from folded paper and opening them to reveal the
design. This form of appliqué is a sophisticated
fabric version. Traditionally, Hawaiian quilts are made
in bright red or blue, often on a white background.

1 Cut a square of
freezer paper to the
size of your finished
background. Fold it in
half, then in quarters,
then fold it diagonally
to form a triangle.

2 Draw an intricate
wavy line around the
folded edges of the paper.
This line includes the appliqué
seam allowance. Cut along the
line, through all layers. Try out
several paper patterns until you
are satisfied with the design.

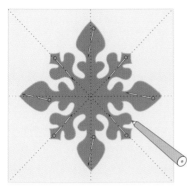

3 Cut a square of appliqué fabric ½in (12mm) larger all around than the paper pattern. Fold and press the fabric into quarters, then into a triangle. Open it out. Press the paper pattern onto the fabric, matching the creased lines. Mark around the edge of the design onto the fabric with a marker pen. Remove the paper and cut out the fabric along the line.

4 Press the background fabric into quarters, then into a triangle. Pin and baste the appliqué to the background along the fold lines, with right sides up, smoothing the fabrics as you go. Baste the appliqué ⅜in (9mm) from the edges of the motif.

5 Beginning close to the center of the motif, turn under a narrow seam allowance with the point of a sharps needle and slipstitch the appliqué to the background. Use your left thumb to hold the appliqué firmly.

6 When you reach a point, stitch to the tip, then trim off the seam allowance. Use the needle to tuck under the seam allowance on the other side of the point. At an inner corner, clip the seam allowance, and take a few extra stitches across the point before continuing along the other side.

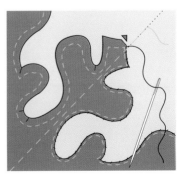

Shadow appliqué

Tip For a first attempt, work with a stiff fabric such as organdy or net.

This delicate technique involves marking a semi-transparent organdy, voile, organza, or net fabric with an appliqué shape and stitching it to a background fabric, then trimming the excess fabric away close to the stitching.

1 Trace a motif onto freezer paper and cut it out. Cut two pieces of transparent fabric in different colors. Use a water-soluble fabric marker to draw around the freezer-paper template onto one of the transparent fabrics. Baste the fabrics together, aligning the straight grain. Place the fabrics in an embroidery hoop.

2 Use embroidery thread to buttonhole stitch (see below) all around the design through both fabrics, ending with a few backstitches on the wrong side. Keep the stitches small and neat. Remove the fabric from the hoop. On the wrong side, trim away the excess fabric close to the stitching line, using sharp embroidery scissors.

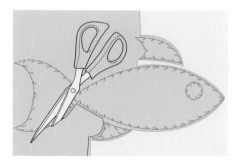

BUTTONHOLE STITCH

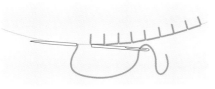

1 Work from right to left. Knot the thread and bring it through to the right side of the fabric, then make a backstitch.

2 Make a second backstitch over the first one, this time bringing the needle out to the left and diagonally above the marked line. Insert the needle directly below, in the hole made by the previous backstitch, then make another backstitch along the marked line. Continue in the same fashion. To finish a row, take the thread to the back and make a few backstitches.

BY MACHINE

Trace the design onto tracing paper, but do not cut it out. Place two transparent fabrics, one on top of the other, and baste the tracing paper on top. Machine stitch the design through the paper and fabrics, using straight stitches, then zigzag over this line. Carefully tear away the paper. Turn the work over and trim the fabric close to the stitching line.

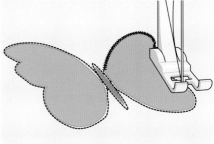

Stained-glass appliqué

Bold designs outlined in black give the effect of a leaded church window in this form of appliqué. The raw edges of the pieces are covered with bias tape. If you are working with straight lines only, ribbon makes a good substitute for the bias tape.

Tip Avoid using small pieces in your design, because it will be hard to shape the bias tape around them. And don't use any "floating" motifs—every piece should have a line connecting it to the next shape.

1 Choose a bold, simple design where all the pieces interconnect. Trace the design onto a cotton foundation fabric and number each piece. To work out how much bias tape will be needed, lay string over the marked lines of the design.

2 Trace the pieces of the design onto the matte side of freezer paper, marking on each the piece number and an arrow for the fabric grain, then cut them out. Press them to the right side of the appliqué fabric, matching the straight grain arrow. Mark around the edges of the freezer paper templates onto the fabric and cut them out.

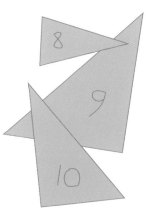

3 Baste the fabric pieces right side upward on the foundation fabric.

4 To make the bias tape, cut 1in (2.5cm) strips on the bias (diagonal) of the fabric. Fold the strip in half lengthways and stitch a ¼in (6mm) seam. Trim the seam allowance to ¹⁄₁₆in (1.5mm).

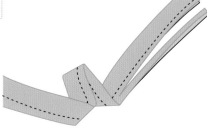

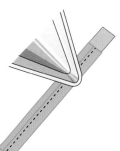

5 Roll the tube so that the seam lies at the center and press it flat, with the seam allowances to one side (inserting a press bar, see *page 19*, will make this easier).

6 Pin lengths of bias tape to the foundation to cover the fabric joins. Where possible, arrange the tape so that the raw ends of one piece can be covered by another strip. Stitch them in place.

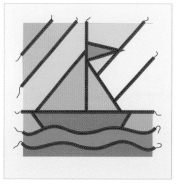

Reverse appliqué

Instead of applying a motif to a background, reverse appliqué works the opposite way, and involves removing part of the top layer of fabric to reveal the material beneath. Three layers are shown here, but you could use just two.

BY HAND

Tip Finely woven cottons are best for beginners; you can turn under the seam allowance without fraying.

Trace the motif onto freezer paper and cut it out. Cut three pieces of fabric, the same size, on the straight grain. Use a quilter's pencil or water-erasable pen to draw around the freezer-paper motif onto the top layer of fabric. Place the fabrics in layers, right-side up, and pin them together. Baste all around the design, ½in (12mm) outside the marked line.

2 Cut away part of the top layer, ¼in (6mm) inside the marked line, using sharp, pointed scissors. Clip inner curves almost to the marked line. Turn under the seam allowance and slipstitch through all the layers. At inner corners, clip the seam to the point and make a couple of extra stitches to prevent fraying. At the outer corners, trim the excess seam allowance before turning under and stitching.

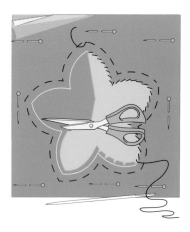

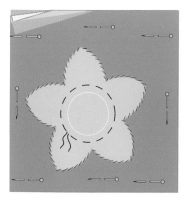

3 Continue cutting and stitching until the design is complete. Remove the basting. Draw a second, smaller motif onto freezer paper to fit within the first motif, and cut it out. Mark the design on the fabric and baste (see step 1).

4 Cut and stitch the fabric to form the motif as in step 2, clipping the curves. Remove the basting. If you wish to remove bulk from the finished design, turn to the wrong side and trim the excess layers of fabric close to the motifs.

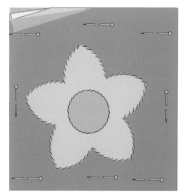

Reverse appliqué

BY MACHINE

1 Prepare the fabrics and mark the design as on page 130 step 1. Instead of basting the fabrics around the edge of the design, baste them with a horizontal and vertical row of stitches.

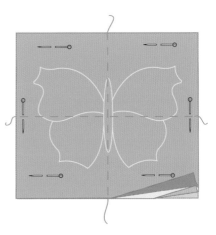

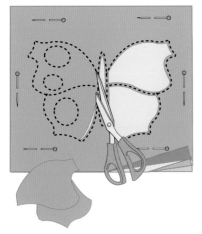

2 Machine stitch over the marked lines using a straight stitch. Cut away the top layer of fabric, just within the stitching line, using sharp embroidery scissors.

Tip Take a practice run at zigzag or satin stitch before stitching your design. Use the same fabrics as your main design, and stitch through three layers, to get an accurate result.

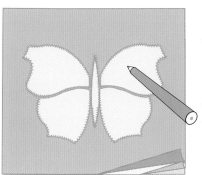

3 Experiment on scrap fabric to get the stitch width and length correct, then satin stitch or zigzag over the straight stitching, covering the raw edges. Use freezer-paper templates, or freehand drawing, to mark the smaller parts of the design within the first motif.

4 Follow steps 2 and 3 to stitch and cut the small motifs. If the end result is too bulky, turn the work to the wrong side and trim away the excess fabrics close to the motif.

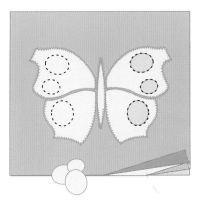

Inserts
You can also insert small pieces of fabric beneath slits cut in the top layer of the appliqué. Reverse appliqué them in position, using the hand-stitch method.

Appliqué designs

You can either use these designs actual size or enlarge them on a photocopier. Seam allowances are not included. Not all appliqué work requires seam allowances, but if they are needed, you can add them when you cut the fabric. If you intend to repeat the motif many times, trace it onto template plastic, or glue your paper copy onto lightweight cardboard and cut it out carefully.

Appliqué designs

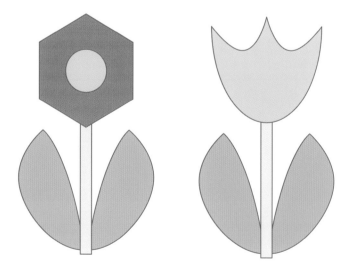

Appliqué designs

QUILTING

QUILTING

A patchwork quilt gets its strength from the rows of

careful small stitches called quilting, and without them

pieced patchwork would not last long. The quilting

protects the seams and holds the filling in place.

Hand quilting requires practice, while machine

quilting is good for speed, but gives your project

less of a hand-crafted finish.

Templates and stencils

Tip If you are making a quilt from patchwork blocks, you will need to piece them together and add borders before quilting (*see page 181 onward*).

You can either buy ready-made stencils and templates for marking your quilting designs, or you can make your own. The latter option gives you the chance to express your own creativity and customize your designs.

TEMPLATES

These plastic shapes have notches or marks for repositioning the stencil. Draw around the stencil onto the fabric, then reposition the template and mark again, to make repeats for a background design or border. For quilting purposes, you can use a geometric template or a motif such as a heart or leaf.

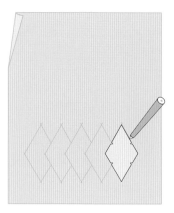

I Draw around the template onto paper or fabric using a marker. Use the notches on the template to position the next section of the design.

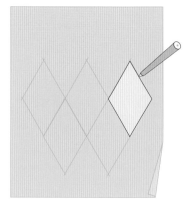

2 To make a border of repeating patterns, use the edge of the previously drawn motif as a guide for positioning the next motif.

STENCILS

Scrolls, waves, flowers, leaves, hearts, and other motifs, as well as background designs of diamonds and lattices, are all available as precut stencils. The stencils have a slit around the outline of the motif to draw through. Position the stencil on the fabric and use a fine marker to draw through the slits. Remove the stencil and fill in the gaps in the design.

CUTTING STENCILS

You can design and cut your own stencils, using motifs from photographs or drawings. Children's coloring books are a good source of simple shapes to copy. Make the stencils from stencil plastic, cutting the channels with a snap-blade knife. Choose straightforward designs, and simplify any parts of the motif that would prove difficult to cut.

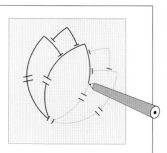

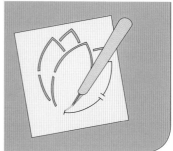

1 Trace the design onto the stencil plastic, marking the position of the slits. You will need to provide "bridges" of uncut plastic, otherwise the stencil will fall to pieces.

2 Put the stencil onto a cutting mat and use a snap-blade knife to cut the slits as marked. A double-bladed X-Acto knife will cut a 1/8in (3mm) channel.

Enlarging designs

The simplest way to enlarge designs is to use a photocopier. If you opt for this method, check the measurements of the photocopied designs carefully, because the photocopier can distort them slightly. Working out your design on graph paper is slower, but will be accurate.

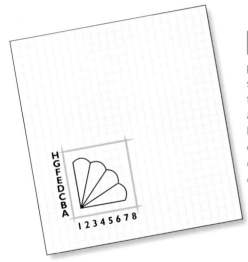

1 Trace or draw your original design on graph paper, matching the main straight lines to a line on the grid. Mark numbers along the bottom edge and letters along the vertical edge, allowing one number or letter per marked square on the graph paper.

2 Take a new piece of graph paper, and mark out the numbers and letters again. This time each number or letter equals two squares (this will double the size of your design; numbering every fourth square would quadruple the size). Now draw the design again, working out the position of the design from the numbers and letters of the grid. For example, the vertical line runs from A1 to H1.

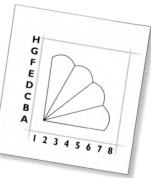

POSITIONING THE DESIGN

To position a quilting design on the quilt top, you can use the seam lines of the patchwork blocks as guidelines or judge the placement by eye. For an accurate result, follow the method below. Some designs can be marked out as you quilt, a little at a time. If your design includes borders and corner motifs, work these out on paper so that you can make any adjustments before marking the quilt top.

1 Trim the graph paper so that it is one square larger than the marked design on all sides. Fold the paper in half, then in quarters, and mark the lines with a pencil.

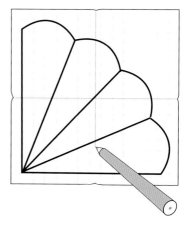

2 Fold the fabric in quarters and mark the center by basting two rows of stitches. Match the penciled center point on the graph paper to the basted center point on the fabric.

Transferring the design

Direct tracing, a lightbox, templates, stencils, masking tape, and carbon paper can all be used to transfer your design to the fabric prior to quilting.

Tip *You need a clear line to quilt over, but it must not show when you have finished. Select your fabric marker with care (see page 20), and press lightly so as not to leave a permanent mark on the fabric. Check the fabric marker on a spare piece of fabric first.*

DIRECT TRACING

This method works for light-colored fabrics. Draw or trace your design onto paper. Go over the drawing with a black marker pen. Tape the fabric over the paper and trace the design, using a fabric marker.

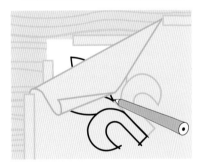

LIGHTBOX METHOD

Tape the paper design to the lightbox, then tape the fabric on top. Trace the design onto the fabric using a fabric marker. You can also tape the design to a window, making use of natural daylight.

PRICKING AND POUNCING

This is a traditional, but more time-consuming method for transferring designs. You can reuse the tracing several times, if you wish to repeat motifs.

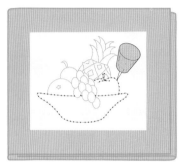

1 Trace the design onto tracing paper, then put it right-side down onto a folded towel or other padded surface. Use a needle with its eye embedded into a cork to prick along the marked line. Alternatively, put a large needle into your sewing machine and stitch around the design without any thread. Rubbing the right side with sandpaper will help to open up the holes.

2 Turn the tracing to the right side and tape it to the fabric. Dip a roll of folded felt or a cotton ball into pounce powder (crushed chalk) and rub over the design, forcing the powder through the holes.

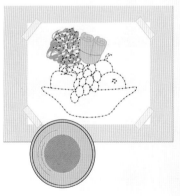

3 Remove the tracing paper and use a quilter's pencil to fill in the dotted line.

Transferring the design

MASKING

Masking tape makes a good temporary marker to quilt alongside, if your design is made up of straight lines. Look for narrow ¼in (6mm) masking tape in quilt shops. Position the masking tape on the quilt top and follow the edge of the tape as you stitch by hand or by machine. The ¼in (6mm) tape is perfect for outline quilting (see *page 157*).

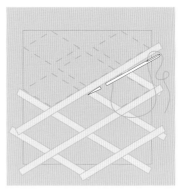

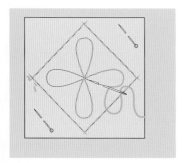

TRACE AND BASTE

This method works well for bold designs and for fabrics that are difficult to mark. You can do it by hand, as shown here, or use the machine version on page 159.

1 Draw or trace your design onto tracing paper. Pin the tracing in position on the fabric. Starting with a knot and a backstitch, work running stitches along the marked lines, through the paper and the fabric. End with a double backstitch.

2 Tear away the tracing paper carefully, leaving the stitches in place. If the paper is hard to remove, score with the point of a needle along the stitching line.

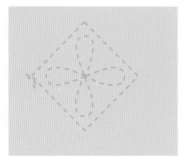

masking tape

tracing paper

DRESSMAKER'S CARBON PAPER

Choose a color that will show up on
your fabric, but be sure to mark the
fabric lightly. Any pressure on the paper
from your hand will leave smudges on
the fabric.

1 Tape the fabric right-side
up to a desk or table.
Place the tracing on top,
taping it temporarily along
one side. Slip the carbon
paper beneath the tracing
and secure it with tape.

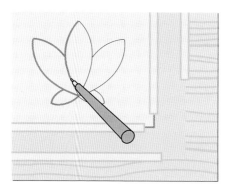

2 Trace firmly over the
marked lines with a
ballpoint pen or tracing
wheel. Do not lean your
hand on the tracing, or
marks will be transferred
to the fabric.

Preparing the quilt sandwich

Once you have marked the quilting design, you must put together the quilt top, the batting, and the backing—known as the "quilt sandwich"—before quilting.

BACKING
Choose a cotton quilt backing of the same weight as your quilt top. If you are a beginner, a printed backing will disguise inexpert quilting stitches. Once you are experienced, however, a plain backing is good for showing off your stitches.

BATTING
Synthetic polyester batting is easy to use, and can be washed or dry-cleaned. Needle-punched polyester is a firmer version. Cotton, silk, and wool are natural choices, but pay heed to any washing instructions. See page 15 for further detail on types of batting.

ASSEMBLING THE QUILT SANDWICH

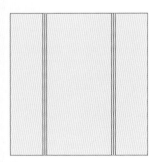

1 Trim off the selvages, then cut the backing 2–4in (5–10cm) larger all around than the quilt top (or 1in/2.5cm larger if you are making a cushion). If you need to seam pieces together to make the backing big enough, place the larger section in the middle, with the seams toward the edges. Press the seams open and flat. Place the backing face down on a flat surface. Smooth it out and check it is square. Tape the edges to the surface to hold it still.

2 Cut the batting slightly smaller than the backing, and place it centrally on top of the backing, smoothing it from the center outward. If you need to make joins, put them at the sides rather than the center. Butt the joined edges together without overlapping them, and join them with a large herringbone stitch. To do this, take a stitch from right to left through the lower piece of batting; make a similar stitch on the upper piece of batting, further to the right.

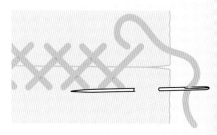

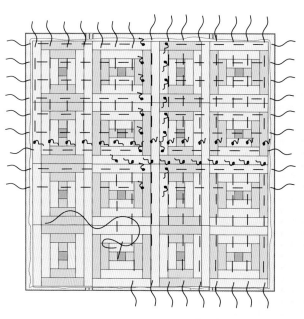

3 Center the quilt top on top of the batting, right-side up. Make sure that it lies flat. Use quilter's safety pins to pin the layers together ready for basting (see overleaf).

Basting the quilt sandwich

Tip For extra security, work diagonal rows of basting across the quilt from one corner to the other.

Baste the layers together so that they do not shift while you quilt. On large projects, a basting gun (which fires plastic tacks) or safety pins can speed up the process.

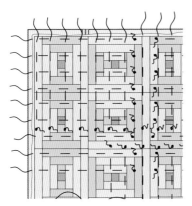

Use thread in a contrasting color and an embroidery or crewel needle. Cut a long piece of thread. Starting from the center, work a row of 2in (5cm) basting stitches to the top edge. Starting again from the center, work another row to the lower edge. Now work further horizontal and vertical rows, spacing them about 3in (7.5cm) apart.

BASTING WITHIN A FRAME

A small project can be basted in a hoop or frame, so that it is ready for quilting.

Cut the backing fabric large enough to fit the hoop or frame. Mount the backing fabric in the hoop, then place the batting and quilt top on the top. Smooth the fabric, then pin and baste as above.

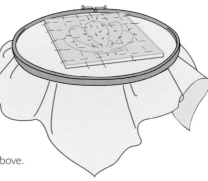

Envelope method

This envelope method makes a quick way of forming the quilt sandwich and finishing the raw edges of a quilt.

1 Place the quilt top wrong-side up on a flat surface. Place the batting on top, smoothing it out carefully. Baste the layers with rows of vertical and horizontal stitches.

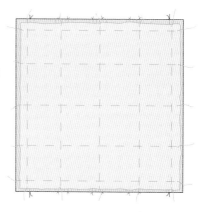

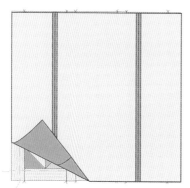

2 Cut the backing to match the quilt top. Place the backing and quilt top together, with right sides facing. Pin and baste, then stitch a seam around all the edges, leaving a large gap of around 10in (25cm) in one side. Trim the corners, and trim the excess batting from the seam line.

3 Turn the quilt to the right side and slipstitch the gap. Baste the three layers together as shown opposite.

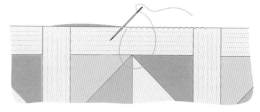

Hoops and frames

Using a hoop or frame when quilting helps to keep the fabric square and the tension even.

HOOPS

Hoops come in circular, oval, and D shapes. On small projects the hoop may cover the entire design. For large designs, be prepared to move the hoop as you work, and take care not to damage worked areas with the hoop. Binding the inner hoop will help to avoid these problems.

1 Wind a bias strip of fabric diagonally around the inner hoop. Sew the ends together, making an even, flat join.

2 Adjust the screw on the outer hoop so that it fits over the inner hoop, with the quilt in between. Press the hoops together, and tighten the screw.

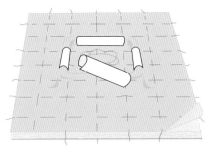

TUBULAR FRAMES

Tubular plastic frames consist of a frame made of plastic piping to go beneath the quilt, and sections of tube that clamp onto this frame, on the right side of the quilt.

STRETCHER FRAMES

If you're working on smaller projects, use a stretcher frame (which is similar to a picture frame). The wooden frame has sides of varying lengths, so choose ones to fit your project.

Fit the frame together and mark the center point of each side. Mark the edges of the quilting in the same way.

Working at the top edge, fasten the center point with a drawing pin, then work out toward the corners. Repeat for the bottom edge, making sure the fabric is taut. Pin the two sides in the same way, stretching the fabric evenly.

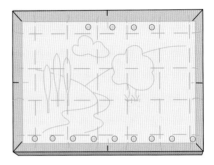

FLOOR FRAMES

A floor frame will keep the tension even on the quilt while you stitch.

| Baste the quilt to the fabric aprons that are attached to the rollers. Now roll the quilt around one roller until it is taut.

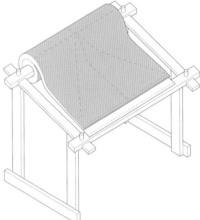

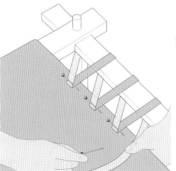

2 You can now attach tape or fabric strips to the side edges of the quilt, using pins, to keep the sides taut.

Hand quilting

For best results, transfer the designs carefully to the quilt top, baste the quilt sandwich together thoroughly, and use a hoop or frame to hold the work. Running stitch is the preferred way to quilt. It's a quick method that produces good results on the back of the design as well as the front. Work from the center outward, completing one section at a time. It's more important that the stitches are even than small. If the project is a cushion, the stitches won't show on the wrong side.

THREAD
Use a thread to match the fiber content of the fabric, which will usually be cotton. Quilting thread is ideal, because it is slightly thicker than standard thread. Draw the thread through a block of beeswax before you start stitching, and use a "betweens" needle.

THIMBLE
When hand quilting, most quilters prefer to wear a thimble on the middle finger of the top hand; some also wear one on the first finger of the hand beneath the quilt, to guide the needle back through the quilt. Wedge the eye of the needle in the end of the thimble, then rock the needle up and down to pick up several stitches.

RUNNING STITCH

Work stitches from right to left
(unless you are left-handed),
making them even on the back
and front of the work. Rock the
needle, and you should be able to
pick up several stitches at a time.

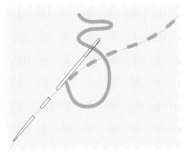

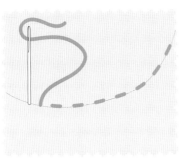

STAB STITCH

Work one stitch at a time,
bringing the needle vertically
through the layers.

STARTING AND ENDING

Start the row with a knot,
and take the needle through
the quilt top into the batting
and back out. Give the thread
a sharp tug and the knot will
disappear into the batting.
At the end of a row, take a
backstitch through the top
and batting only, then run
the needle into the batting
and bring it to the surface.
Pull the thread and cut it
close to the fabric surface.
The thread end should
disappear into the quilt.

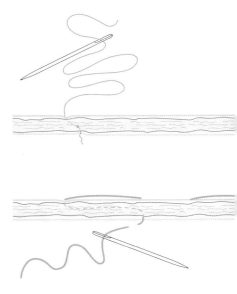

Quilting hints

Most people find hand quilting enjoyable, and it's easy to get into the rhythm of stitching.

- The back of the quilt should look as good as the front, so check as you work that the stitches go through all three layers. With practice, your stitches will get smaller.
- Aim for an even tension, without causing the fabric to pucker. If you are having problems, check that the tension in your hoop or frame is not too tight, and adjust it until the fabric is quite slack.
- To quilt the outer edges of a project that won't fit neatly into the hoop, baste strips of scrap fabric to the edges of the project before placing it in the hoop.
- Sit close to a table and rest the edge of the hoop against it, so that you don't have to support the work while you stitch.
- To stitch across several layers, such as seam allowances, use stab stitches rather than running stitch.
- If you are stitching rows, it may be easier to thread several needles and work in sections across the quilt.
- Following the seam lines of the quilting, or working random stitches, are alternatives to stitching elaborate quilting patterns.

wooden hoops

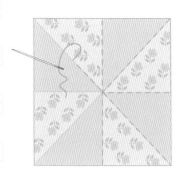

QUILTING IN THE DITCH

Quilt along the seam lines within each block to hold the quilt securely without adding decorative lines of quilting.

OUTLINE QUILTING

Follow the seam lines of the block, but quilt ¼in (6mm) on either side of the line to outline them.

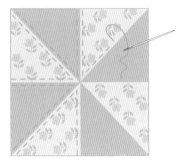

ECHO QUILTING

Make a row of quilting close to the edges of a motif, then continue with further rows, each one evenly spaced from the previous row.

SEED QUILTING

Small straight stitches worked in all directions give an allover effect and can be used to make a motif stand proud of its background.

Machine quilting

Layer and baste your quilt carefully for successful machine quilting. Make a test run on scrap fabric layered with batting and backing. Use an even-feed foot and set a straight stitch. Stitch a few rows, adjusting the stitch length if necessary.

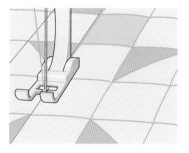

To machine quilt in the ditch, follow the seam lines of the patchwork (see *diagram*). To outline or echo quilt, follow the hand quilting method on page 157. For echo quilting, use the machine foot as a guide for stitching subsequent rows.

STITCHING A GRID

1 Mark the quilt from top to bottom, through the center point. Attach an even-feed foot and quilting guide to your sewing machine and stitch the marked center row.

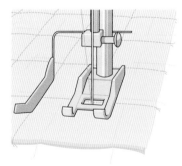

2 Stitch the next row to the right of the first, aligning the bar of the quilting guide with the first row of stitches. Make further rows until you reach the edge.

3 Attach the quilting guide to the right of the machine foot, and stitch the rows to the left of the center point.

4 Use exactly the same method to work horizontal rows.

> **Tip** When starting and finishing rows at the center of your quilt, do not work reverse stitches, but leave long thread ends to finish by hand later on.

FREE QUILTING

Use a darning foot and lower the feed dogs on the machine. Set the stitch length and width to 0. Lower the presser bar and take a stitch to bring both threads to the surface. Start stitching, moving the fabric to create curves. For vermicelli stitching, make tiny loops and curves covering the whole surface.

COUCHING

Thread embroidery yarn through the hole in a braiding or embroidery foot. Work narrow zigzag stitches to cover or "couch" the embroidery thread.

> **Tip** Roll up the quilt so that it fits under the arm of the sewing machine.

TRACE-AND-TACK QUILTING

Baste the quilt layers together as on pages 150–151. Transfer your quilting design to tracing paper, and pin the tracing to the quilt through all layers. Machine stitch over the marked line. Then tear away the tracing paper.

Quilting designs

Designs for quilting range from straightforward motifs and simple borders to the most elaborate forms of swags, leaves, feathers, and medallions. These intricate patterns are shown to best advantage on wholecloth quilts (where the top of the quilt is one piece of fabric, with the design in the quilting pattern), rather than stitched onto colorful pieced blocks, where the designs would tend to get lost.

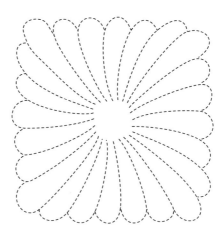

Quilting designs

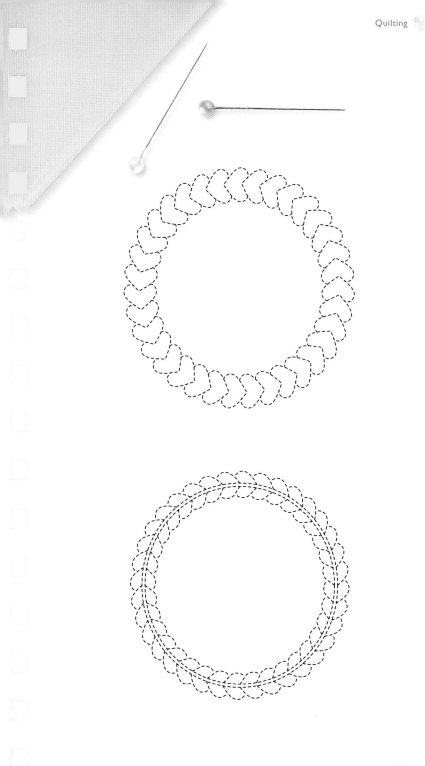

Quilting designs

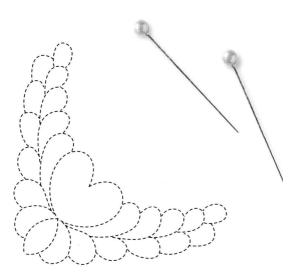

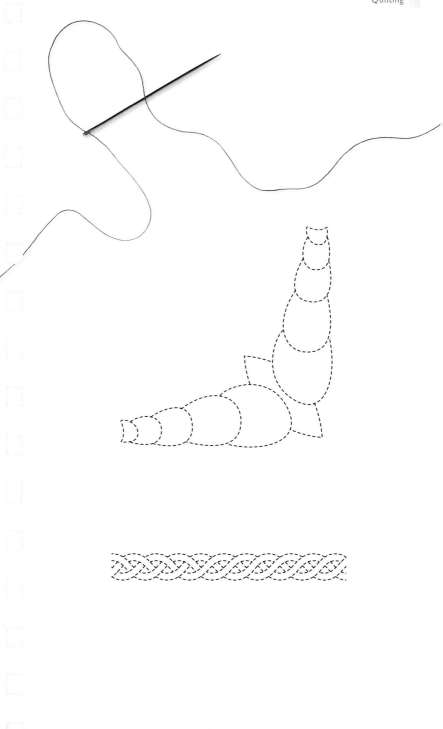

Quilting designs

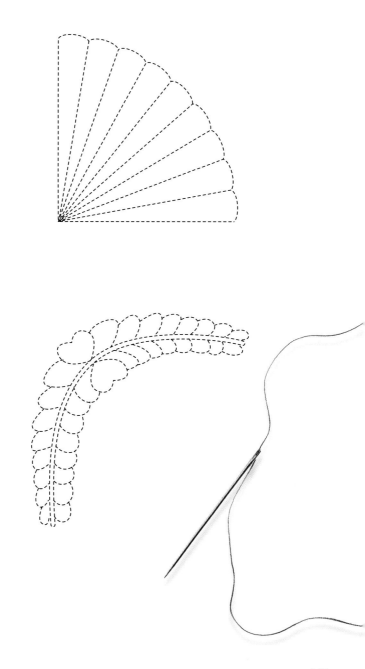

Quilt and sew

This piecing technique (*see pages 78–79*) uses a foundation fabric topped with batting so that you can piece as well as quilt at the same time.

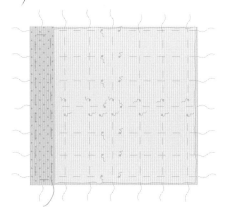

1 Place the foundation fabric on a flat surface and baste a piece of batting on top. Pin and then baste the first foundation strip, right-side up, on the left edge of the foundation and batting, matching the raw edges.

2 Place a second strip over the first one, with right sides together, and stitch the right edge through all layers. Flip the second strip open, then add a third strip in the same way. Continue until the piece is covered.

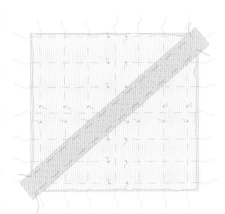

3 To work a diagonal design, place the first strip across the foundation and batting from corner to corner. Place a second strip over the first, and stitch along the left edge. Flip open and continue to the edge.

4 Turn the work around and attach further strips from the center outward, until the whole piece is covered.

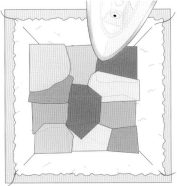

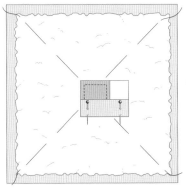

5 Use the same technique to make crazy patchwork and log cabin patchwork, starting from the center and working outward.

Quilt as you go

Use this method to quilt pieced blocks individually before putting them together to make a quilt.

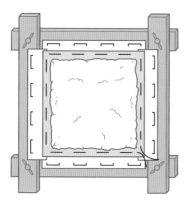

1 Cut the backing fabric 1in (2.5cm) larger than the block. Staple fabric strips to a frame, and baste the backing fabric to the strips. Place the batting and then the finished block right side up on top, and baste the layers together.

2 Quilt the block by hand (see pages 154–157). If you are quilting close to the edge of the block, you will need to join the blocks using strips (see page 172). Otherwise, leave a ½in (13mm) unquilted border.

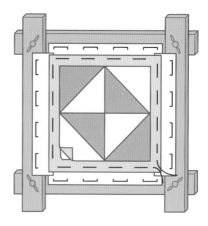

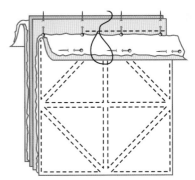

JOINING BLOCKS

1 Place blocks with right sides matching and pin the top layers together. Fold and pin the batting and backing out of the way. Stitch a ¼in (6mm) seam.

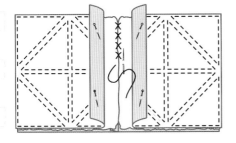

2 Open the blocks and use a finger to press the seam to one side. Remove the pins from the batting and smooth it over the top layer, trimming it so that the edges meet. Use large cross stitches to hold the batting in place.

3 Smooth one piece of backing fabric over the batting and fold the other edge on top, tucking under a ¼in (6mm) seam allowance and finger pressing. Slipstitch the backing fabric together.

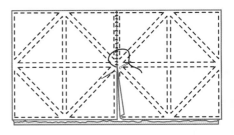

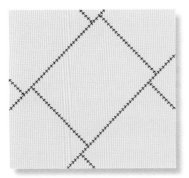

4 Continue piecing the blocks to form a row. Join the rows together in the same way.

More joining methods

You can use narrow strips to join the blocks, or if you wish to make a quilt with sashing (*see pages 184–187*), use the method below to pad the sashed strips.

STRIP JOINING

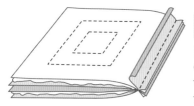

1 Cut a strip from backing fabric the length of the block and 1¼in (3cm) wide. Press a ¼in (6mm) hem on one long edge. Pin two blocks together, right sides facing, and pin the strip on top with the raw edges matching. Stitch.

2 Open out the joined blocks. Trim the seam allowances to remove the bulk and fold to one side, then fold the free edge of the strip to cover the join and slipstitch in place.

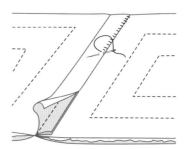

SASHING

Cut sashing strips the length of the block and the desired width, adding ¼in (6mm) seam allowance to each side. Cut the batting ¼in (6mm) smaller all around than the sashing strips. Baste the batting to one sashing strip. Pin this sashing strip to the right side of the block, and another strip (without batting) to the wrong side of the block, and stitch together.

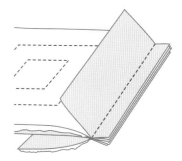

2 Open out the padded sashing strip and stitch it to a second block.

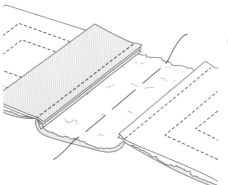

3 Fold the raw edge of the sashing strip to cover the batting. Fold under the seam allowance and slipstitch in place. Continue in this way to make a row of sashed blocks, then use long sashing strips to join the blocks together.

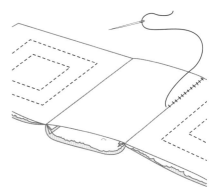

Sashiko

Tip Use a thick thread, such as cotton perle.

The Japanese art of quilting was once designed to strengthen fabric, and was later employed as a decorative technique. Use longer stitches than in normal quilting and choose thread in a contrasting color. For ease of stitching, use a thin batting. The designs were originally stitched in white on an indigo-dyed fabric.

TRADITIONAL METHOD

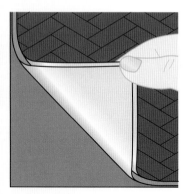

1 Draw out your design full size on graph paper. Transfer the design to the fabric using dressmaker's carbon paper (*see method on page 147*). Place the backing, a thin batting, and the top layer together and make rows of basting through all the layers.

2 Study the design to work out an order of stitching that allows long, continuous rows without breaking the thread too often (*see opposite*). Starting with a concealed knot between the layers, work continuous rows of running stitch with 5, 6, or 7 stitches per inch (2.5cm).

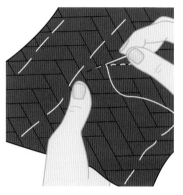

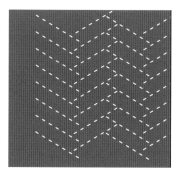

3 Keep the stitches even and long, and do not overlap them where rows of stitching meet.

BY MACHINE

You can also work Sashiko designs by machine. Transfer your design to the backing fabric. Thread the machine with a top-stitching thread in the bobbin, and stitch with the right side of the quilt downward. Putting the "top" thread in the bobbin reduces the strain on the thread. Do not worry about leaving gaps where rows of stitching meet (as you would with hand stitching)—simply stitch over the joins.

FINDING A STITCHING LINE

For both hand and machine Sashiko, the work is easier if you are not constantly breaking off the thread to start a new part of the design.

SHIPPO

Look out for long stitching lines within this Shippo design.

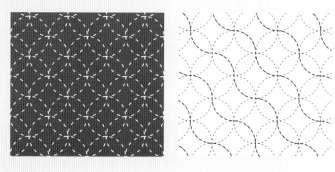

Sashiko designs

Sashiko patterns include simple, repetitive geometric and curved designs, and some more involved grids. Many patterns are inspired by nature.

PARALLEL DIAMONDS

Parallel rows of stitching emphasize the diamond pattern.

UROKO FISH SCALES

This is one of the oldest Sashiko patterns and is still popular.

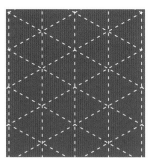

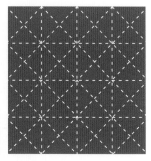

OVERLAID CHECK

Antique garments have been found featuring the overlaid check pattern.

FUNDO COUNTERWEIGHTS

This pattern is based on the weights used in market scales.

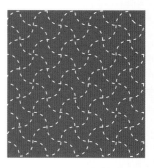

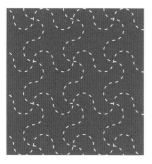

CHIDORI

This design symbolizes the sea-birds called plovers. Its name means "thousand birds."

MIST

It's easy to conjure up the mist represented by this pattern.

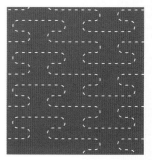

Sashiko designs

INAZUMA LIGHTNING

There are several variations of this popular lightning design.

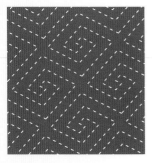

PAMPAS GRASS

The shapes here are similar to the clamshells shown earlier in this book.

HEMP LEAF

Hemp leaf is often stitched on clothing for small children.

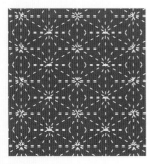

Tied quilting

Much faster than standard quilting, tied quilting gives a soft, puffy effect and you can include more filling layers.

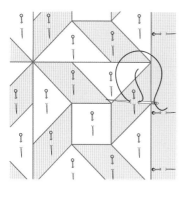

1 Assemble the quilt layers and pin them together, placing a pin where each tie will go (place them every 6in/15cm). Using thick thread such as crochet or cotton perle, thread a needle and make a backstitch across the pin, through all layers, leaving a 2–3in (5–7.5cm) tail. Make a further backstitch over the first one and cut the thread, leaving a long tail as before.

2 Tie the tails in a knot: first right over left, then left over right. Trim the tails evenly.

FAST TIES

Work backstitches as above, and do not cut thread, but leave it loose between each pin. When you reach the end of the thread, cut and tie knots as before.

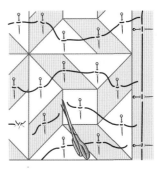

Bows, buttons, and tufts

Tip Make ties every 6in (15cm) or, if you intend to wash the quilt regularly, place the ties every 3in (7.5cm).

Give your quilt a fancy finish with some decorative ribbon bows or tufts, or some smart buttons, for that extra flourish.

BOWS

Use either decorative thread or fine ribbon. Leave long ends, and tie in a double bow.

BUTTONS

Stitch the buttons to the quilt, securing them at the front or at the back with a knot.

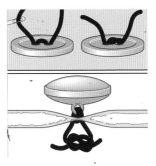

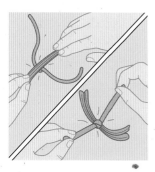

TUFTS

Follow steps 1 and 2 on page 179, leaving 5in (12.7cm) tails, then lay three strands of yarn, each 2in (5cm) long, over the knot. Tie a second reef knot to secure them.

SETTING AND FINISHING

SETTING AND FINISHING

Now that you've pieced your project, it's time to show

it to best advantage. Here's how to assemble blocks

and use sashing strips to accentuate the design of a

quilt. There are various bindings to protect the edges,

and embellishments such as prairie points, all of which

will make your project into a work of art to treasure.

Setting

The "set" of a quilt is the way the blocks are arranged. This is one of the most creative parts of quilt making, and blocks look surprisingly different depending on their orientation.

STRAIGHT SETS

In straight sets, blocks are arranged in identical ordered rows.

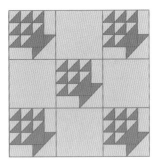

PLAIN AND PIECED

You can alternate pieced blocks with plain squares (this is called setting squares).

BUILDING BLOCKS

Turning blocks around creates a four-block design.

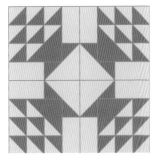

MEDALLION

Nine-patch blocks are here combined with setting squares to make a medallion.

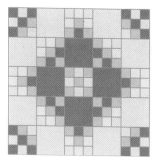

BLOCKS ON POINT

Rotating the blocks so they stand on their corners creates quilt designs on the diagonal. Blocks are stitched in diagonal rows, and setting triangles are added at the ends to fill in the gaps.

PLAIN AND PIECED ON POINT

You can alternate plain and pieced blocks to make the pieced blocks stand out.

Sashing designs

Adding sashing strips between blocks lets them stand alone without crowding their neighbors. It's useful for unifying blocks that wouldn't normally sit happily together.

STRAIGHTFORWARD SASHING

Use this set to emphasize the repeat block design.

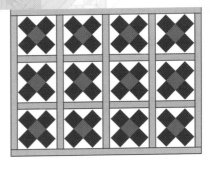

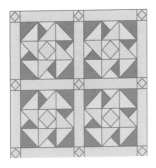

PIECED SQUARES

You can piece the small setting squares between the sashing to add interest to your design.

VERTICAL SASHING

Add vertical sashing strips to a fruit-basket design.

DIAGONAL SET WITH SASHING

Sashing works well when blocks are set on point, too.

STRIP QUILT

Some motifs, such as flying geese, lend themselves to piecing in strips rather than blocks.

ADDITIONAL BORDERS

Add both plain and pieced borders to emphasize your design.

Sashing

Using strips of fabric to divide the quilt blocks can unify your quilt design. The plain sashing strips act as a background to the pieced blocks, highlighting the patterned work.

CONTINUOUS SASHING

1 Cut long sashing strips to the desired width plus ¼in (6mm) on each side for the seam allowance. Cut the long strip into pieces of the same length as the edge of an unfinished quilt block. Arrange the strips and blocks as shown and, with right sides together, sew the strips to the blocks, taking a ¼in (6mm) seam. Press the seam allowances toward the sashing.

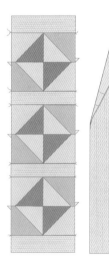

2 Cut further sashing strips to fit the length of a row of pieced blocks and strips. With right sides together, stitch the sashing strip to the row of blocks. Press the seams toward the sashing.

3 Continue to stitch sashing strips to the rows of pieced strips and blocks to complete the quilt.

SASHING WITH CORNER SQUARES

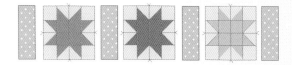

1 Decide on the width of the sashing strips, adding ¼in (6mm) on each side for the seam allowance, and cut long strips. Cut the strip into pieces of the same length as the edge of an unfinished block. With right sides together, stitch a sashing strip to either side of the blocks, taking a ¼in (6mm) seam allowance. Press the seam allowances toward the sashing.

Tip If possible, cut strips along the lengthwise grain. They are less stretchy than crosswise strips.

2 Cut corner squares the same width as the sashing strips. Stitch the squares to either side of the sashing strips, as shown. Press the seams toward the sashing strips.

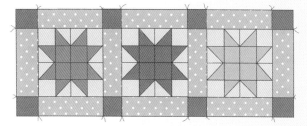

3 Stitch the rows of sashing and blocks to the rows of sashing and corner squares to make up the quilt.

Borders

A border not only protects the edges of the quilt, but can show it off to best advantage. Cut border strips along the lengthwise grain of the fabric.

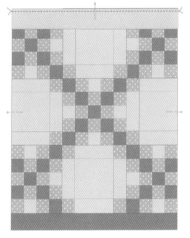

STRAIGHT BORDERS

1 Cut border strips to the desired width plus ½in (12mm). Cut two strips to fit across the top and bottom of the quilt. Mark the center of the strips with pins. Stitch the strips to the top and bottom of the quilt, matching the pins to the center of the quilt. Press the seams toward the border strip.

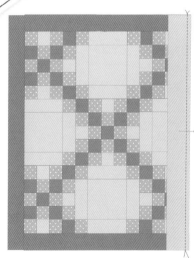

2 Cut two strips to fit the length of the quilt (including the stitched top and bottom borders). Mark the center of each strip with pins. Stitch the borders to the sides of the quilt, matching the pins to the center of the quilt. Press the seam allowances toward the border strip.

MITERED BORDERS

1 Cut border strips to the desired width plus ½in (12mm). Cut the strips to the length of each side of the quilt plus two border widths plus 2in (5cm). Mark the center of each border and the center of the quilt edge with a pin. Place a further pin ¼in (6mm) from the corner of the quilt.

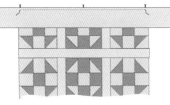

2 Match the pins and stitch the first border to the quilt, stopping and starting at the outer pins. Stitch the other borders in the same way.

3 Turn the quilt right-side up and fold under the loose end of one border strip at a 45-degree angle. Fold the other strip so that they meet. Press.

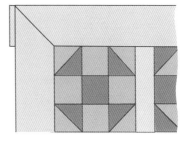

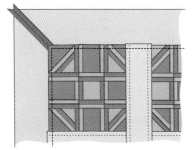

4 Turn the quilt over and fold it diagonally from the corner, matching the folded border edges. Pin, baste, and stitch the seam from the corner of the quilt top to the outer edge. Trim the seam allowance to ¼in (6mm). Press the seam open. Repeat on each corner to complete the quilt.

Binding

Binding encloses all the raw edges of a quilt, giving it a secure finish. Single binding is good for small wall hangings; double binding is stronger and ideal for bed quilts, but it is bulkier.

BEFORE BINDING

Trim the quilt top, batting, and backing so that the edges are even, and baste the layers together around the edges. If you baste within the seam allowance, you will not need to remove the basting later.

SINGLE-FOLD BINDING

1 Cut binding strips on the crosswise grain of the fabric (from selvage to selvage), twice the desired finished width plus ½in (12mm) for seam allowances. Cut the strips slightly longer than the quilt edges, joining pieces with a straight seam if necessary.

2 With right sides together, match the raw edge of the binding to a side raw edge of the quilt. Stitch, taking a ¼in (6mm) seam. Turn the binding to the wrong side, turn under ¼in (6mm), and slipstitch to the back of the quilt. Trim the ends even with the quilt. Repeat at the other side.

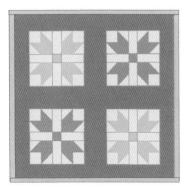

3 Bind the top and bottom of the quilt in the same way, folding under the excess fabric at the ends to neaten the corners. Slipstitch the folded edges at the corners.

DOUBLE-FOLD BINDING

Double-fold binding is made from a strip of fabric folded lengthwise to make two layers.

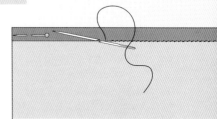

1 Cut binding strips on the crosswise grain of the fabric, making them four times the desired finished width plus ½in (12mm) for seam allowances. Fold the binding in half lengthwise, with wrong sides together. Cut the strip slightly longer than the side edge of the quilt (join strips if necessary, taking a straight seam). Match the raw edges of the binding to the edge of the quilt front and stitch, taking a ¼in (6mm) seam.

2 Fold the binding to the wrong side and slipstitch the folded edge to the backing, following the seam line. Trim the ends to match the quilt edge. Bind the other side edge in the same way. Bind the top and bottom, following step 3 above.

Mitering corners

Mitering the corner seams of double-fold binding creates a neat finish.

1 Make up enough binding to fit all around the quilt plus 15in (38cm). Pin the binding to one quilt edge (not starting from a corner), matching the raw edges. When you reach a corner, stop stitching ¼in (6mm) before the edge. Backstitch and remove the quilt from the machine. Fold the binding straight up over the seam just sewn, so it is parallel to the edge of the quilt.

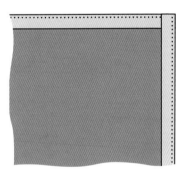

1

2 Now fold the binding straight down, matching the raw edges and maintaining the fold in the binding at the corner. Start stitching ¼in (6mm) from the corner. Continue around the quilt, and when you reach your starting point, stop sewing 4in (10cm) away from it. Fold the two binding ends so that they meet at a 45-degree angle, and then finger press them. Stitch them together at the fold and trim the ends. Stitch the binding to finish the seam.

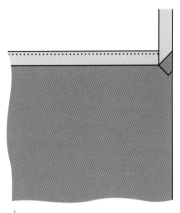

2

3 Fold the binding to the back of the quilt and slipstitch into place. Slipstitch across the miter at each corner.

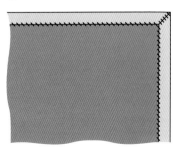

3

Bias binding

Curved-edge quilts need to be bound with bias binding, which has enough flexibility to fit neatly around the curves.

1 To decide on the binding width, see pages 190–191. Cut bias strips from the fabric at a 45-degree angle. To find the correct angle, fold the raw edge to the selvage and mark the diagonal.

2 Join strips of bias binding by stitching the short ends together at a diagonal. Press the seam allowance open. Make a strip long enough to surround the quilt plus 10in (25cm).

3 Fold the binding in half lengthways, with wrong sides together. Pin and stitch the raw edges of the binding to the quilt, with right sides facing and raw edges matching, taking a ¼in (6mm) seam (see step 2, page 190). Clip the edges of the binding around tight curves, if necessary. Stitch the folded edge of the binding along the seam line. Tuck and and stitch the short raw edges when you reach the join.

Foldover binding

If you cut the quilt backing rather larger than usual,
you can fold the edges over the quilt front, forming
a mock binding.

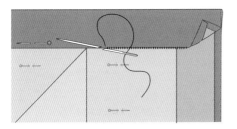

1 Cut the quilt backing
3–4in (7.5–10cm)
larger all around than
the quilt top (for small
projects, cut the backing
1in/2.5cm larger). Spread
the backing wrong-side
up on a flat surface or the

floor, then center the batting and quilt top on top, right-
side up. Turn and press a ¼in (6mm) hem on the edges
of the backing. Fold the pressed edge to the right side
along the top of the quilt, then slipstitch to the quilt.
Repeat for the quilt bottom.

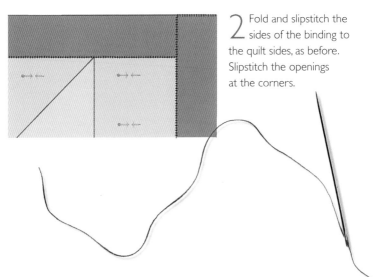

2 Fold and slipstitch the
sides of the binding to
the quilt sides, as before.
Slipstitch the openings
at the corners.

Piping

This corded finish gives a crisp edge to cushions or bags.

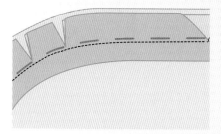

1 Cut a bias strip of fabric (see page 193) twice the width of the cord, plus ½in (12mm). Fold the strip around the cord, right side outward, and baste close to the cord.

2 For an unquilted project, baste the piping to the quilt front, clipping the piping edges around tight curves. Using a zipper foot or piping foot, machine stitch close to the piping.

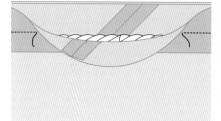

3 Where ends of piping meet, stitch the ends of the bias strip together (see page 193). Cut the cord ends so that they butt against each other, then stitch them together. Fold the strip over the cord and stitch.

4 Place the backing and quilt top with right sides together, and stitch all around, leaving a gap. Turn to the right side and slipstitch the opening. For a quilted project, stitch the piping to the quilt front, folding the backing and batting out of the way. Turn to the wrong side, fold under the raw edges of the backing, and slipstitch to the seam line of the piping.

Ruffles

Extend the size of your cushion or baby quilt by adding some soft ruffles.

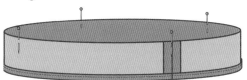

1 For the ruffle length, measure all around the edge of the project and multiply by two. For the width, choose your desired width and add ¾in (18mm). Cut a fabric strip this size. Stitch the short ends, right sides together. On one long edge, turn and press ¼in (6mm), then turn again and stitch to make a double hem. Mark the ruffle into quarters using pins.

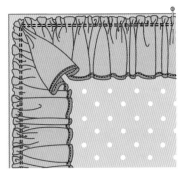

2 Make two rows of gathering stitches along the remaining raw edge, either side of the ¼in (6mm) seam line. Use pins to mark four equidistant points on the project edge. Draw up the gathers. For an unquilted project, baste the ruffle to the quilt top, with right sides together, matching the pins.

3 Baste the backing fabric to the quilt top, with right sides together and the ruffle sandwiched between them. Stitch all around, leaving a gap. Turn through to the right side. For a quilted project, stitch the ruffle following step 4 on page 195.

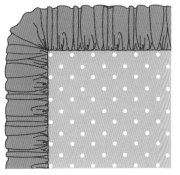

Prairie points

These useful little triangles make a pretty edging to finish off a quilt. You can also use individual points to add accent and color to a project, inserting them into a seam before you stitch it.

NESTING PRAIRIE POINTS

1 Cut 2in (5cm) fabric squares. Fold the squares in half diagonally and then press.

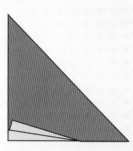

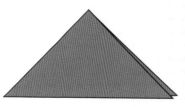

2 Fold the resultant triangles diagonally in half again and press.

3 Slip each triangle inside the fold of its neighboring triangle, then pin them together to make a row.

Prairie points

OVERLAPPING PRAIRIE POINTS

1 Cut 2in (5cm) fabric squares. Fold each square in half to form a rectangle and press. Bring the corners of the folded edge to meet at the center point of the lower edge, forming a triangle, and press.

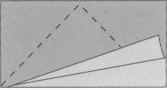

2 Place a row of triangles with their points touching, then place a second row on top of them, matching the center seam on the front triangle with the two points of the triangles at the back. Pin to form a row.

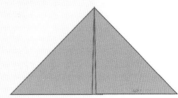

Making insertions in a seam

Use this method for attaching prairie points, covered cording, ribbon, or lace into a seam to decorate a quilt or cushion.

Tip When pinning praire points to the quilt top, adjust the distance between the triangles so that you finish with a completed point at each corner.

I Pin and baste the prairie points or other trimmings to the right side of your project, with raw edges matching. Pin the backing fabric to the project front, with right sides facing and raw edges matching. Stitch the seam. If stitching all four sides of a quilt or cushion, you will need to leave a gap in the seam to turn the project through to the right side after stitching.

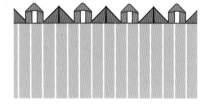

2 Turn through to the right side. The embellishments now decorate the edge of the project. If you left a gap for turning through, slipstitch it closed.

Method for quilted projects

If you have already quilted your project, follow this method to attach the prairie points or other insertions. Baste the row of triangles (or other insertion) to the right side of the quilt top, folding the backing and batting out of the way. Continue along the sides and bottom, then stitch, taking a ¼in (6mm) seam. Turn the quilt over, and turn under ¼in (6mm) on the backing. Slipstitch in place.

Ribbon ruffle

Embellish a quilt top with a quick-to-sew ribbon ruffle. It can be stitched in place either by hand or by machine.

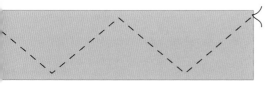

Choose a medium or wide ribbon. Set the sewing machine to a long straight stitch, then stitch long zigzags along the length of the ribbon.

2 Draw up the top thread and the ribbon will form gathers, as shown.

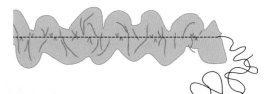

Bias tubes

This handy technique makes a tube that can be wound into spirals and curves to decorate the surface of a quilt.

Fold the fabric diagonally and mark the diagonal. Use this mark as a guide to cut a 1in (2.5cm) bias strip. Cut the strip to the length required, fold it in half lengthwise with right sides together, and stitch ¼in (6mm) from the folded edge. Using strong cotton, thread a large needle and make secure backstitches at one end of the fabric tube. Push the needle, eye first, through the opening.

2 Tug the needle gently, and ease the fabric tube through to the right side.

2

Yo-yos

Stitch these circular motifs to your project to decorate it, or stitch yo-yos together to make an openwork quilt or cushion cover.

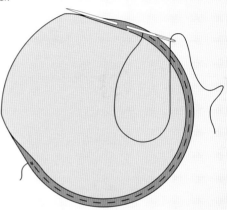

1 Draw around a plate or saucer, or use a pair of compasses on tracing paper or freezer paper, to make circles just over twice the diameter of your finished yo-yo. Cut out the paper templates, and use them to mark circles on the fabric. Cut the circles out. Fold ¼in (6mm) to the wrong side all around the edge and, starting with a knot, work running stitches over the folded edge, all around the circle. Overlap the first and last stitches.

> **Tip** If you want to use yo-yos of different sizes, stitch them to a background fabric in a contrasting color. To pad the yo-yos, cut a circle from batting the size of a finished yo-yo, and place it on the fabric circle before drawing up the edges.

2 Pull up the thread to gather the fabric. Finish with several backstitches. Press the circle flat.

Glossary

A

Amish patchwork A style developed by the Amish people, using simple geometric shapes.

Appliqué Stitching fabric shapes to a background.

B

Backing The fabric layer that forms the back of a quilt.

Backstitch Formed by taking stitches both backward and forward along a row to create a continuous row of stitches on the surface.

Basting Long stitches that hold fabric layers together ready for stitching.

Basting gun Inserts plastic tacks to hold a quilt sandwich together.

Batting The padding used inside a quilt.

Between A short needle that is used for quilting.

Bias strip A strip cut diagonal to the fabric grain, used for binding.

Binding Used to protect the edges of a quilt.

Blanket stitch A stitch used for the edges of blankets and decoratively in patchwork.

Blind stitch Small, neat stitches that are virtually invisible.

Block A unit composed of patchwork pieces, usually square. Blocks are combined to form a quilt.

Border A fabric frame around a quilt.

Broderie perse An appliqué technique using motifs cut from printed fabrics.

C

Cathedral window A folded patchwork technique involving "frames" made from foundation fabric, folded around insert "windows."

Chain piecing Stitching pairs of patches by machine, one after another without stopping.

Charm quilt A quilt composed of fabric pieces where no two pieces are the same.

Clamshells Shell-shaped pieces stitched in overlapping rows to a background fabric.

Couching A thick embroidery thread laid on the surface of the work and held in place by tiny stitches.

Courthouse steps A version of log-cabin patchwork.

Crazy patchwork Randomly cut shapes stitched to a foundation fabric.

Cross stitch Use for embroidering and to hold batting pieces together.

Cutting mat Used for rotary cutting (see rotary cutter).

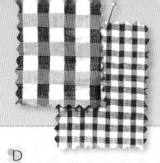

D

Dresden plates Applied patchwork using fabric segments to form a circular motif.

Dressmaker's carbon paper A paper available in various colors with a special finish, used to mark fabrics.

Drunkard's path A popular curved patchwork design.

E

Echo quilting Quilting parallel to the edge of a motif to echo its shape. Several consecutive rows may be used.

English piecing Fabric shapes stitched over paper patterns, worked by hand.

F

Feed dogs The mechanism beneath the sewing-machine needle plate that moves to push the fabric along.

Finger press Using a thumb and finger, or a fingernail, to crease a fabric without an iron.

Five-patch block A block made up of 25 individual squares.

Folded star Folded fabric triangles arranged consecutively to form a star.

Foundation A fabric base onto which other pieces are stitched.

Foundation piecing Pieces stitched to a background, either along marked seam lines or at random.

Four-patch block The most common patchwork block, made up from pieces always divisible by four.

Frame A wooden or plastic holder used to stretch fabric taut.

Freeform quilting Quilting without a pattern.

Freezer paper Paper with a coating that sticks temporarily to fabric.

Fusible interfacing A fibrous fabric that bonds to a fabric piece when pressed with an iron.

Fusible web A web of fibers that melts when heat is applied, to fuse fabric layers together.

G

Grain The direction of the woven warp or weft threads of a fabric. The lengthwise grain follows the direction of the selvages; the crosswise grain runs from selvage to selvage.

H

Half-square triangle A triangle made by cutting a square diagonally in half.

Hawaiian appliqué A bold, intricate motif, usually in bright colors, appliquéd to a foundation fabric.

Hoop Two closely fitting circles or ovals of wood, used to keep fabric taut while stitching.

In the ditch Rows of quilting following the seam lines of each block.

Isometric paper A graph paper for drafting patchwork shapes, using equilateral triangles instead of squares.

Log cabin A type of patchwork consisting of strips stitched in order around a central square.

Marking Transferring a design onto fabric.

Miter A neat angled join where borders meet at the corners.

Needle-turn appliqué The point of the needle is used to turn under appliqué edges while stitching.

Nine-patch block Nine squares pieced together to form a block.

Outline quilting Quilting that follows the seam lines of a block at a ¼in (6mm) distance.

Patchwork Small pieces of fabric stitched together to create a design.

Piecing Joining patches together to form a block.

Prairie points A row of triangles used to edge a quilt.

Press bar Used to press bias tape flat.

Pricking and pouncing Transferring a design using a perforated tracing and powdered chalk.

Quarter seamer Marks a ¼in (6mm) seam allowance.

Quarter-square triangle Formed by cutting a square on both diagonals into four triangles (see half-square triangles).

Quilt and sew Patchwork that is stitched and quilted all in one to a foundation.

Quilt as you go A method for quilting blocks individually before joining them.

Quilting stencil A stencil with grooves for marking a design.

Quilting stitch A running stitch that holds the layers of a quilt together.

Rail fence A strip-piecing design.

Raw-edge appliqué Stitching appliqué pieces in place without turning a hem.

Reverse appliqué Removing layers of fabric to reveal a design.

Right sides together Placing fabrics with the fronts facing each other.

Rotary cutter A sharp, circular blade fixed in a holder, used with a cutting mat for speed cutting.

Rotary ruler A clear plastic ruler marked with ¼in (or 6mm) divisions.

S

Sashiko Japanese quilting, usually worked in white running stitch on an indigo background.

Sashing Strips of fabric inserted between pieced blocks to make borders.

Satin stitch A close zigzag stitch usually worked by machine.

Seed quilting Small, straight stitches worked in all directions.

Selvage The finished edge of a bolt of fabric.

Seminole patchwork An intricate patchwork of pieced strips that are cut up and repieced to form patterns.

Setting The arrangement of blocks and borders to form the quilt top.

Setting in Joining fabric pieces by stitching one shape into the angle of another shape.

Seven-patch block A block made up of 49 equal squares.

Shadow appliqué Appliqué using transparent fabrics.

Sharps A long fine needle, good for tacking a quilt together and for appliqué.

Slipstitch Small stitches designed not to show on the right side of the work.

Stab stitch A running stitch made vertically through fabric, one stitch at a time.

Stained-glass appliqué The application of black bias strips to border colorful pieces.

Straight grain Usually the lengthwise grain, but can refer to the crosswise grain.

String patchwork Using narrow strips of leftover fabric to create a design.

Strip piecing Cutting and stitching strips rather than individual patches, used for speed.

T

Template A plastic, paper, or card shape for drawing around onto fabric.

Tied quilting Uses ties instead of quilting stitches to hold quilt layers together.

Turn through Turning joined fabrics to the right side through a gap left in the seam.

W

Warp The threads that run the length of the fabric.

Weft The threads that run across the fabric from selvage to selvage.

Whipstitch An oversewing stitch used to fasten two edges together.

Wholecloth quilt A quilt comprising one large piece of fabric to form the top, elaborately quilted.

Window template A template of the outline of a patchwork shape for marking the finished size and seam allowance.

Y

Yo-yo A circular motif made from gathered fabric circles.

Index